Nicolette Loizou

T0268392

111 Pl
in Cante~~~~~bury
That You
Shouldn't Miss

(111)

emons:

© Photographs by Nicolette Loizou, except:
Bagpuss (ch. 2): Nicolette Loizou, with special thanks to the Firmin
and Postgate families for granting permission to photograph Bagpuss;
British Cartoon Archive (ch. 3): Special Collections and Archives,
University of Kent; Canterbury Cross (ch. 7): © Canterbury Museums
and Galleries; World War II Forts (ch. 111): Matthew Barnes Whitstable
Boat Trips www.whitstableboattrips.co.uk; author headshot: Holly Chapman
© Cover icon: © Canterbury Museums and Galleries
Layout: Eva Kraskes, based on a design
by Lübbeke | Naumann | Thoben
Maps: altancicek.design, www.altancicek.de
Basic cartographical information from Openstreetmap,
© OpenStreetMap-Mitwirkende, OdbL
Editing: Alison Lester
Printing and binding: Grafisches Centrum Cuno, Calbe
Printed in Germany 2022
ISBN 978-3-7408-0899-0
First edition

Did you enjoy this guidebook? Would you like to see more?
Join us in uncovering new places around the world on:
www.111places.com

Foreword

From the bell towers and sky-high cliffs right down to the depths of the London Clay marshlands, this part of Kent has a story everywhere. Reminders of England's past, its wars ancient and modern, industries rising and declining, are found across field, forest and shore.

There were once 52 pubs in Whitstable. Great days! A quiet fishing village reinvented as a foodie's delight, staying true to itself by giving a spirited 'no thanks' to the chains, Whitstable has welcomed Londoners for decades, sometimes referring to them as 'Down From Londoners', DFLs for short. But who can blame the capital's escapees? Growing up in Kent, it took time in London for me to appreciate the world I had left behind. I won't make this mistake again.

Herne Bay has transformed itself from sleepy outpost to a *costa* steeped in English eccentricity. Where else, I challenge you, can you find a bakery selling frog-shaped cakes, a broken pier and a flag-decorated army surplus shop? Grab your chips and make that windswept walk to mysterious Reculver. I have done this since I can remember and am now increasingly conscious of what it would be like if this – and our other fragile seaside treasures – were ever to disappear under the waves.

Canterbury's spookiness is hard to resist. Heads under beds, unexplained Roman bones, mysterious swords and bombed-out buildings are just some of the stories. Chaucer, Marlowe and Somerset Maugham weaved both evil and good into their fictional tales. But Canterbury is also a fun city, offering both wonky old buildings and modern ones filled with cartoon history. Even its natural landscape brings a smile with a comically bizarre tree and fruits destined for warming cider. Curio shops burst with antiques, sweet treats abound and it is also the forever home for Rupert the Bear and the adorable Bagpuss. And for me too.

111 Places

1 All Saints Lane

Saved from the wrecking ball

You'll have to look carefully for some of Canterbury's best-preserved timber-framed buildings, as they are very easy to miss. This tucked-away enclave is only 60 metres in length and features a handful of venerable buildings gathered in a pretty row. All Saints Court shines as its extremely well-preserved star attraction. Formerly a pilgrims' rest associated with nearby Eastbridge Hospital, it was turned into five cottages in the 18th century before degrading into slums. One of these cottages, All Saints Cottage, is a highly sought-after guest accommodation. Visitors have to adapt to the winding staircase and sloping floors that will transport them back to 1500, the year it was built, nine years before Henry VIII took to the throne and continued the tempestuous reign of the Tudors.

You can't go inside and view its 30-metre-long floor, the longest in Canterbury and once put to optimum use for a dancing school, but check out the steeply pitched tiled roof with a large central brick stack and weatherboarded end gables, and don't miss its most stunning features – the intricate carved brackets in the form of fearsome beasts glaring out with contorted faces.

Declared unfit for habitation in the 1920s, All Saints Court was listed for demolition by the council, until builder Walter Cozens, son of the founder of the Canterbury Historical & Archaeological Society, stepped in and organised its restoration, revealing its current frontage. Cozens senior (buried in St Martin's churchyard, see ch. 12) would have been proud, as he was instrumental in the development of many Canterbury landmarks such as the original Simon Langton Schools (lost in the Baedeker raid of 1942). His legacy can be spied via the city's Cozen's commemorative paving stones which are easy to miss. Surviving into modern times with hardly any modern signs, the ancient buildings of this rare area of quiet invite you to stop, exhale and allow yourself to be transported far back in time.

Address CT1 2AU | Getting there 12-minute walk from Canterbury West station via St Peter's Street; Queningate car park | Hours Exterior unrestricted | Tip Turnagain Lane off Palace Street reveals another hidden Canterbury treasure. Amongst the medieval buildings includes one with a third storey added in the 17th century.

2__Bagpuss
Those mice are never serious!

Beloved of Generation X is saggy Bagpuss, who brought just 13 stories of whimsy and kindness to 1970s children's television.

The frequently yawning pink-and-white cat is displayed here looking good in his dotage and still exuding a lovable placidity. Created by Canterbury locals Oliver Postgate and Peter Firmin, the cuddly feline was the favourite toy of a little girl named Emily who found lost curios and broken objects and displayed them in her ramshackle shop. Now, of course, she might be tempted to flog them on eBay, but in less commercial times she lived in hope that their owners would come and collect them. Bagpuss negotiated the storyline with the help of a think bubble, and his narratives bumbled along with other characters such as the dry Professor Yaffle, who was based on philosopher Bertrand Russell, and the excitable mice (also on display here). The level of imagination led to the show being hailed as a classic, and Firmin and Postgate have been the subject of numerous retrospectives.

Pre CGI, Bafta-winning Firmin and Postgate used an animation technique called 'stop motion' to create the programme's gentle style. It was a truly local endeavour – the team set up their business in a disused cowshed surrounded by pigsties at Firmin's home in Blean, just outside the city. Their company, Smallfilms, also dreamed up such other classics as *Noggin the Nog* and *The Clangers*. As testimony to the enduring imagination of Postgate, *The Clangers* delights a fresh generation of children today, although it has been rebooted for digital times.

Yet it is *Bagpuss* that today's grown-ups still hold dear, and here he is preserved forever in the city where he was born. In 1987, when Postgate was awarded an honorary degree at the University of Kent, his co-creator stated that the accolade was really for the cat that had charmed a generation.

Address The Beaney House of Art and Knowledge, 18 High Street, CT1 2BD, +44 (0)1227 862162, www.canterburymusuems.co.uk | **Getting there** 8-minute walk from Canterbury West station via St Peter's Street and onto the High Street; Canterbury West station car park | **Hours** Tue–Sat 10am–5pm, Sun 11am–4pm | **Tip** Craving real cats? Head to William Street in Herne Bay for a visit to the Cosy Cat Café and enjoy a hot drink and the company of its rescued animals.

3 British Cartoon Archive
Political pot-shots saved for posterity

Hidden away in a warren-like department in the University of Kent is a place sparkling with humour and insight, where you can delve into boxes packed ceiling-high that reveal a nation's modern history captured in pen and pencil. Now considered to hold the largest collection of political cartoons in the country, this comic chronicle came into being by chance. In the 1970s, some of the University's academics with a fondness for Britain's rich cartoon history managed to get hold of a cache of drawings lampooning society and politics and war.

Now part of the University's Special Collection and Archives Department, roughly 200,000 cartoons from the likes of Carl Giles (*Express*) and Martin Rowson (*Guardian/Mirror*) are held here. These satirical pot-shots, dating back to 1904, would have otherwise been consigned to the bin. While the focus is on Britain and the starry names that we are familiar with are all there, there is also work from Egyptian-born Kimon Marengo (1904–1988) who unpicked the treacherous Middle East situation with a dynamite wit. With cartoons tackling all mainstream political persuasions, these drawings showcase the role of the newspaper cartoonist, which is fading sadly alongside the role of the print journalist.

The collection's team of dedicated archivists are currently undertaking the mammoth task of digitizing this material. But you don't want to view such stinging satire from behind a screen. Get down there and take a look for yourself. You will need to make an appointment to gain entry, but the effort is worth it. Get these delicate vintage witticisms into your hands.

The archivists are a little vague on the question of the market value of the collection, but they think it is insured to the value of millions. Like all great art, though, they acknowledge that its true worth is priceless. See for yourself.

Address Templeman Library, University of Kent, CT2 7NU, +44 (0)1227 764000, www.cartoons.ac.uk, cartoons@kent.ac.uk | Getting there Unibus or bus 4 to University; parking on site | Hours By appointment only | Tip Fancy creating your own cartoons? Head to family-run George's Mini Market in Whitstable and create your own witty works from its range of art and craft supplies.

4 Buttermarket

From bulls to buskers

Surrounded by commercial trappings of the 21st century, this site would once have been even more buoyant to the tide of market forces. Bustling now, it was positively hectic up to the middle of the 17th century when it was known as the Bull Stake. Bulls were tethered here and held overnight to be 'baited' by dogs, a practice thought to produce more tender meat. The Buttermarket veers off into Butchery Lane where meaty types would slaughter the animals and fishmongers' benches overflowed with catches from nearby waters.

Now uncovered, the Buttermarket was once a much grander affair, complete with an oval canopy and columns. These were demolished in 1888 due to the ravages of time and weather. For a glimpse of its earlier appearance, the Old Buttermarket pub has a sign featuring the market in all its rowdy glory. Previously a coaching inn, flint in the pub's cellars indicates that it may have once stood on Roman remains. It is also suspected that it used to be connected by tunnels to the cathedral. Regulars at the pub are said to have included a raucous nun and a ghostly monk.

The once-covered market was chosen in 1891 to showcase *The Muse of Poetry*, a memorial to Christopher Marlowe (see ch. 31). Twentieth-century master T. S. Eliot stayed at the nearby Cathedral Gate Hotel when his verse drama, *Murder in the Cathedral,* was performed in the cathedral. C. S. Lewis also stayed at the hotel in the 1940s when he was researching for his masterpiece *The Lion, the Witch and the Wardrobe.*

Now the most prominent element of the site is the memorial to those who served in World War I; there is little indication of the literary stars connected with this part of the city. It's also a popular meeting point, and whilst the hubbub of an agricultural market may be long gone, buskers favour this spot for their impromptu songs and protesters occasionally gather here too.

Address Burgate, CT1 2HW | Getting there 10-minute walk through the city centre from Canterbury West station; Queningate car park | Hours Unrestricted | Tip For more on Canterbury's role in conflict there is a 1922 memorial horse trough in the High Street beside the former Nasons. Troughs of these kind commemorating animals killed in war are rare.

5 _ Café St Pierre

Rendezvous dans une pâtisserie parfaite

French Huguenots escaping persecution descended on Canterbury in the 17th century to British welcomes based on a common religion and the opportunity to bridge the skills shortage gap. With time though, this welcome gave way to wariness and suspicion. Today, however, peckish locals as well as French tourists enjoy French culinary talent in this café, situated in an often-overlooked part of the city. The Huguenots are no longer to be found weaving their fine silks and wools in Canterbury but the continental talent for creativity is alive and well here.

Given the choices displayed, you will never go hungry in this small establishment bursting with Gallic charm. With walls draped with French flags and decorated with signs and maps evoking our sophisticated neighbours, the look might be down to shabby-chic aesthetics or, *peut-être*, a refusal to follow the trends of the chain café. The baguettes and eclairs are similarly bursting with the taste of a chic Parisian eatery. Keep sweet with pâtisseries including glossy strawberry tarts and apricot and pistachio cakes or get salty with herby sausage rolls.

There's little chance you would be able to practise your French with a chain barista, but you certainly can here. Have a word with the chef-patron as he carries his trays of fragrant delicacies about, evoking images of a typical French gourmet wearing a striped apron and a somewhat nonchalant expression.

There is a small garden in the back where sparrows hop about for crumbs from the not-always-steady tables, and the coffees arrive promptly. The specials board is changed frequently, and the lack of music makes it ideal for a cosy catch-up. Prices are reasonable too when you consider the quality and freshness. Today's French émigrés in Canterbury provoke British adoration instead of the apathy and suspicion of old. Let us all eat cake.

Address 11 St Peter's Street, CT1 2BG, +44 (0)1227 456791 | Getting there 10-minute walk from Canterbury West station towards the city centre and past Westgate Gardens; Canterbury West station car park | Hours Mon–Fri 8am–6pm, Sat 8am–6pm, Sun 9am–5.30pm | Tip The Beaney House of Art & Knowledge has a few insights from Huguenot times including a bible, woven silk and a mourning ring (www.canterburymuseums.co.uk/beaney).

6_ Canterbury Bookbinders
One of a kind in Kent

You can never have too many books, and Christopher Paveley has handled thousands in his nimble hands at the helm of Canterbury Bookbinders. No, he hasn't read them all, but he knows them inside out, having given them the love and attention they deserve by employing his talent as a bookbinder on this site for the last 30 years. In a ramshackle studio in Northgate he has stitched and hand-sewn leather-bound books using hand-marbled boards and endpapers, creating ways to make books stand out on the shelves.

One part of his business is restoring family bibles for clients locally, nationally and abroad in America, France and Italy who call on his distinct skills for their precious keepsakes. His studio is as quiet as a library and embossed books are piled on top of one another. Above them are rows of hundreds of spiky, brass-plated heirloom tools. They look like they could cause some damage in the wrong hands, but the bookbinder's hands are gentle and flexible, using them purely for the love of transforming books for a prized place in your collection. His hands have tended to valuable volumes dating as far back as the late 1500s. These works were more durable than you might think. Our wise ancestors truly revered the book.

One of his projects involved crafting a book to be presented to Queen Elizabeth by an author who paid £2,500 to please the monarch.

Perhaps you do not have that much money knocking about, but if you would like your novel professionally bound, a rough starting-point figure is £40. Trickier jobs for him include photographic albums, but everything he does is bespoke, and he also tackles the modern world with more commercial projects.

As the last remaining bookbinder of his kind in Kent, Chris is sure that for the future his craft will be called upon to enchant both writer and reader. And we are too.

Address 60 Northgate, CT1 1BB, +44 (0)1227 452371, www.canterburybookbinders.co.uk, canterburybookbinders@hotmail.co.uk | **Getting there** 10-minute walk from the city centre past the Buttermarket; Northgate car park | **Hours** By appointment only | **Tip** Crowthers of Canterbury on the Borough nearby is another small independent shop dedicated to creativity, but this one repairs instruments and includes rare oboes and sheet music (www.crowthersofcanterbury.co.uk).

7 Canterbury Cross
Crossing hearts here and abroad

If ever there was a symbol of a city, it has to be the Canterbury Cross. Cropping up on jewellery, ceramics and even in fashion, it dates from around 850 AD. The Canterbury Cross has acquired widespread fame and is a much-cherished symbol of Christianity. Its distinctive design, slightly reminiscent of a four-leaf clover, is found all over the city and beyond. In 1932, a Canterbury Cross made of pieces of Canterbury stone was sent to all the Anglican diocesan cathedrals of the world as a symbol of communion with Canterbury. But no doubt it's the original you're after, so head to The Beaney House of Art & Knowledge, where the icon has been on display since 2017. You may find it to be much smaller than you expected, given the mighty impact of its design.

Delighted diggers unearthed the cross in 1867 during excavations in St George's Street. Almost nothing is known about its provenance, but the very mystery surrounding it remains part of its appeal. We do know that it was cast in bronze and features intricate decorations in its Saxon design. Note the four silver triangle engravings which are filled with a mixture of copper, silver, lead and sulphur. These would have been expensive materials at the time, so the cross was most likely made for someone of high status. It would have been practical as well as pretty, probably with a pin on the back so it could be worn to fasten a cloak or other garment. Today, it makes its modern mark on contemporary t-shirts as well as the more familiar earrings, thanks to its eye-catching decorative style. The artisan who designed it is unlikely to have been able to imagine its tremendous commercial power, and one wonders if they would have celebrated it being printed onto clothing.

Look out for echoes of it on railings, bollards and gravestones, as well as on the stone cross, familiar to pilgrims, outside the cathedral.

Address The Beaney, 18 High Street, CT1 2RA, +44 (0)1227 862162, www.canterburymuseums.co.uk/beaney | Getting there 8-minute walk from Canterbury West station down Station Road and then left into the High Street until you reach The Beaney; Canterbury West station car park | Hours Tue – Sat 10am – 5pm | Tip Kent was renowned for its talent in jewellery, metalwork and glass. Also, in The Beaney is an Anglo-Saxon dragon pendant which may have been a treasured lucky charm.

8 Canterbury Pottery

The wheels are always turning here

Since the 1960s, this tiny shop and studio has been brightening up the city with trademark ceramics in sea blue and grass green.

With Richard and Jan Chapman in the back throwing pots at their wheels to the soothing hum of Radio 4, it is a quiet respite from the hue and cry of the Buttermarket. Compost containers and garlic holders sit merrily amongst the more standard mugs and plates. The creative couple are directly inspired by the city and surrounding Kentish towns with their oast houses (hop kilns – see ch. 21) as well as their apple and cherry trees. In their words, 'Orchards, hop gardens and stunning coastlines are reflected in our own distinctive glazes.'

The Chapmans also have the cathedral, which almost faces the shop, for a client. Their communion sets are individually decorated with the Canterbury Cross (see ch. 7). Jan says, 'The Canterbury Cross is a beautiful and very distinctive design. I think we're all fortunate in Canterbury to have this lovely symbol. It is particularly suited for our purposes.' Altar candlesticks lighting up the interior of the expansive cathedral are another one of their creations. But you do not have to be an archbishop to take something they make home with you. They also do a range of everything from pretty vases to umbrella stands to Thomas Becket and Black Prince mugs, decorated using a transfer technique. It's funny to think of a medieval military hero making his way onto a piece of pottery, but it might well have suited the prince's lust for self-glorification. Their ceramics celebrating both legendary local figures are sure to keep any tea drinker with a soft spot for history happy.

The Chapmans' ceramics aren't only to be seen cradling garlic or the communion host in Canterbury. Their chalices and patens (small plates used for Mass) have found their way to churches in places as far-flung as Mexico and the Philippines.

Address 38A Burgate, CT1 2HW, +44 (0)1227 452608, www.canterburypottery.com |
Getting there 5-minute walk from city centre towards Buttermarket; Queningate car park |
Hours Mon–Fri 9.30am–5pm, Sat 9.30am–5pm | Tip For more ceramics, head to Cosmo
China for work from Josie Firmin, daughter of the creator of beloved children's characters
such as Bagpuss and Ivor the Engine (www.cosmochina.co.uk).

9 Canterbury Rock

Step into vinyl heaven with a true music fan

'The Japanese think it's a museum,' says Jim Hampshire, the affable owner of Canterbury Rock for 40 years. He mimes them clicking away as Neil Young plays softly. Perhaps it is a museum of sorts, with vintage Smiths and Beatles vinyl racked up against a dusty display of hi-fi equipment, concert posters and signed gig tickets. Jim maintains that this beloved shop is still cramming customers in despite the onslaught of the internet. A true analog man, it is an invention which he steadfastly refuses to use. When I enquire how much some of my old vinyl is worth, he hazards a pretty good guess before consulting one of the many rock bibles he keeps behind the counter. There is even a 7-inch of *God Save the Queen* taking pride of place which is, sadly, not for sale. For the truly archaic, he even sells cassettes.

Fans past and present of the shop include a member of Roxy Music, various session musicians and a certain Guy Berryman from a rather popular band called Coldplay, who studied at Kent College back in the 1990s. 'Someone once rang me asking for David Bowie's number,' says Jim from behind a counter of 1950s retro singles and their glorious covers of coiffed beatniks and swell broads. A vinyl fan, he is hopeful for the continuing health of the shop but is strict with his lunching beliefs (always closed between 12pm and 1pm) and you certainly won't see him here on Sunday. As mainstream record shops hit the wall there is something comforting about this place. You come here to buy but you also come here to chat about tunes with a passionate fanboy who knows his stuff and will fill you in with all manner of recommendations as you browse the racks.

Look out for the drawing at the left of the shop showing a caricature of a goblin ecstatic at his musical haul. That goblin could be any of us after a trip here because you will end up with a discovery or three after a visit.

Address 12 Whitstable Road, CT2 8DQ, +44 (0)1227 458393 | Getting there 3-minute walk from Canterbury West station, turning right toward Whitstable and past the round-about; Canterbury West station car park | Hours Mon–Sat 10.30am–noon & 1–6pm | Tip For more retro rummaging head to Rock Bottom Records in Whitstable.

10_ Chaucer Statue
The pilgrim's progress

You don't have to look very far in Canterbury for reminders of this great medieval writer. The city holds him close to its heart with a hotel, hospital, school, road and even a cheese bearing his name. Yet it was only in 2016, after a ten-year project and much clamour, that the great chronicler had a statue commemorating him in the city. Not only that; it was the first statue of the writer in England at all!

Chaucer wrote *The Canterbury Tales* between 1387 and his death in 1400, and their popularity meant the collection of tales became one of the first books printed at a time of increasing literacy, in 1476. Dressed as a pilgrim gazing in the direction of the East-bridge, a 12th-century place of rest for the pilgrims Chaucer celebrated and satirized in his 24 tales, the writer holds a copy of his legendary work. The printers' blocks for his name are also represented. Kent-based sculptor Sam Holland crafted the statue in bronze, and it stands on a metre-tall plinth crafted in minute detail by Yorkshire-based Lynn O'Dowd, whose frieze is as full of fun as the tales themselves. One of the storytelling pilgrims depicted is the Summoner, who was fond of a drink and had dreadful boils. A more attractive prospect is Canterbury-raised Hollywood heart-throb Orlando Bloom, who is depicted as the Young Squire. Look out for the faces of other local stars.

Chaucer wears an astrolabe quadrant, an early navigation instrument for determining longitude, latitude and time of day via the sun and the stars. It is not a facsimile of the Canterbury Astrolabe Quadrant, the only one known definitively to have been made in England, which was found in a dig at the House of Agnes hotel in 2005 and is now housed at the British Museum. Sculptor Sam Holland instead based it on the one Chaucer described in his 1391 instruction manual, *A Treatise on the Astrolabe*.

Address CT1 2AZ | Getting there 15-minute walk from Canterbury West station via the High Street; Whitefriars car park | Hours Unrestricted | Tip Take a trip to nearby Boughton-under-Blean and the 15th-century White Horse Inn, a coaching inn mentioned by Chaucer in the *Tales*.

11_ Chilham
Where the heart is

Romantic author Jane Austen's heart was captured by Kent, and location scouts looking for sites to film her Regency- and Georgian-set works are captivated too. It's easy to see why Chilham – six miles outside Canterbury – is such a magnet. Timbered Tudor houses and a church that can claim 16th-century origins make up some of the stars of a village that also includes cottages, old-fashioned tea rooms and a farm shop. But they all orbit round the draw that is the landscaped grounds of where Chilham Castle was first established. Here the focus is not romance but science.

The Jacobean revamp of the inhabited house as we see it now was managed in 1616 by Sir Dudley Digges. He might not sound familiar, and nor might his father, Thomas Digges, who introduced England to the solar system as we know it. (But it's hard to be moved by the laws of science when you encounter Chilham today. The BBC filmed their 2009 adaptation of Austen's *Emma* here, and an adaption of Agatha Christie's Miss Marple novel, *The Moving Finger*, also drew on its soft-focus beauty.) Sir Dudley Digges was something of a literary fan himself and was rumoured to be an acquaintance of Shakespeare. A one-time special ambassador to the Netherlands and a commissioner of the East India Company, his global reach extended to Canada and Virginia in the American colonies. Other inhabitants of the estate included a Threadneedle Street banker whose spendthrift son squandered the family fortune. And there was Sir Edmund Davis, who in the beginning of the 20th century made huge profits internationally in coal, tin and chrome. Eccentric inhabitants come and go, but the sweet chestnuts and terrace topiary in the castle grounds remain a constant feature as does the northern part of the 'haha' – a ditch keeping park livestock away from the house without interrupting the views that have captured so many hearts.

Address Chilham, CT4 8DL, +44 (0)1227 733100, www.chilham-castle.co.uk, enquiries@chilham-castle.co.uk | Getting there 10-minute walk from Chilham station; Chilham car park | Hours Exterior unrestricted; limited groups can visit the house if booked in advance; gardens open May–Sep, Tue & Thu 10am–4pm | Tip You may not live in a castle, but you could easily furnish your home in its style with a visit to Bagham Barn Antiques on the Canterbury Road, a restored 17th-century barn housing one of the largest collections of antique furniture, collectables and art in Kent (www.baghambarnantiques.com).

12 ___ Church of St Martin

The oldest church in Canterbury, and beyond

Canterbury may be in the shadow of a different, and very mighty, ecclesiastical building, but this church holds an ace card like no other: it is in fact the oldest church in continuous use in the English-speaking world.

Founded centuries before the divisions between the eastern and western churches and Catholic and Protestant troubles, this church is cheeringly inclusive. Part Roman and part Saxon in architectural style, it should be used as a poster child for peace and harmony. It sits in its own tranquil aura, tucked away from the main thoroughfare of the city and seldom visited by tourists, looking like something out of *Midsomer Murders.*

When Canterbury's first archbishop, Augustine, wrote to Saint Gregory in the 6th century about differing customs in various churches, the wise man replied: 'I wish you to choose carefully and teach the church of the English, which as yet is new to the faith.' This little church was the base from which Augustine's monks pursued their mission to convert Kent to Christianity. They had been inspired by the county's – and England's – first king to convert, the incomparable Ethelbert. Outside, you can see examples of re-used, burnt-red Roman brickwork incorporated into the structure of the south wall. The buttresses at the corners are of a distinctly Saxon style. Some of the stone was imported from near Paris.

Legend has it that St Martin's was used as a chapel for ancient Kent royalty, and Ethelbert himself was probably baptized here in 597. However, the county's monarchs were not interred here and instead were buried at nearby St Augustine's Abbey. Amongst the romantic idyll of the churchyard lies a sizable amount of Commonwealth war graves as well as the final resting place of Rupert Bear creator Mary Tourtel and celebrated local artist Sidney Cooper (see ch. 46). They certainly withdrew to a place of peaceful repose.

Address 1 North Holmes Road, CT1 1QJ, +44 (0)1227 768072, www.martinpaul.org, office@martinpaul.org | Getting there 10-minute walk from the city centre, via Longport; on-street parking in North Holmes Road and St Martin's Avenue | Hours Usually Tue, Thu, Fri & Sat 11am – 3pm, but consult website for updates; churchyard unrestricted | Tip Nearby on Lower Chantry Lane are long, lean almshouses built by John and Ann Smith in 1657. The gables reflect the architectural influence of Dutch Protestant immigrants escaping historic persecution.

13 City Cemetery

I love the smell of lavender in the morning

The great writer Joseph Conrad who penned *Heart of Darkness,* familiar to millions via the 1979 movie based on it, *Apocalypse Now,* is
associated with some of the most exciting places in the world via his
timeless works. Yet he is rarely associated with Canterbury, or rather
the village of Bishopsbourne, four miles outside the city, where he
lived from the end of 1919 until his death in 1924. He and his family
entertained a great deal at the house, hosting many lunch and dinner
parties, and the Village Hall is referred to as Conrad Hall.

Despite his influence, his grave in Canterbury Cemetery attracts
few on the literary trail. It is not signposted and is somewhat hard
to find (section 'N' at the far north-east of the cemetery) amidst the
maze of ornate graves.

Here in this peaceful area, which dates back to 1877, the spell of
the city's shops feels far away. The double chapel in the middle of the
cemetery is surrounded by fragrant lavender and features rag stone
with Bath stone dressings indicating superior craftsmanship. And
you cannot miss its 110-foot spire, a rarity in the city, which guides
you towards the cemetery. Two small stone heads greet you at the
entry to the chapels and their likeness to Ethelbert and Bertha (see
ch. 27) is particularly strong.

As for the seafaring writer's grave, it is a Grade II listed monument, but the local sculptor got his name wrong, engraving his
middle name as Teador and not Teodor. It was not the only affront
for the author of *The Secret Agent.* The Ukrainian-born writer had a
funeral procession through the city where his friends noted that he
did not receive the recognition he deserved. And as his last journey coincided with Cricket Week, sporting fans held up the procession. But maybe the writer with ironic tendencies would have
seen some strange humour in the surrounding jollity as his hearse
spluttered along.

Address Westgate Court Avenue, +44 (0)1227 862 490 | **Getting there** 12-minute walk from Canterbury West station via Station Road and St Dunstan's Street; Queningate car park | **Hours** Pedestrian access unrestricted; road gates open Mon–Fri 8.30am–4.30pm | **Tip** Aphra Behn attracted considerable attention for her raucous 17th-century plays, poetry and novels featuring well-rounded female characters. Baptized in hilly Harbledown near Canterbury, her impact on the English novel is undeniable.

JOSEPH TEADOR CONRAD
KORZENIOWSKI
BORN DECEMBER 3RD 1857
DIED AUGUST 3RD 1924

SLEEP AFTER TOYLE, PORT AFTER STORMIE SEAS
EASE AFTER WARRE, DEATH AFTER LIFE DOES GREATLY PLEASE
SPENSER

JESSIE EMMELINE CONRAD
KORZENIOWSKA
BORN FEBRUARY 22ND 1873
DIED DECEMBER 6TH 1936

14__Conquest House
A murder is announced

The one historical moment which is best known as inextricably linked with Canterbury is surely the murder of Thomas Becket, Archbishop of Canterbury from 1162 until his death in 1170. The cathedral was the scene of the audacious, history-changing crime, but you can visit 8 Palace Street, the location of the attractive half-timbered Conquest House, where the nefarious plan was hatched.

As archbishop, Becket established himself as a thorn in the side of Henry II, with the one-time chess partners clashing about clerical privilege. Thomas Becket steadfastly defended the church and angered the monarch so much he fled to France for his own protection. Becket's time away did not calm the waters, however. He remained outspoken, and the king is alleged to have cried, 'Will no one rid me of this turbulent priest!' Taking this as a summons to assassination, four of Henry's knights left immediately for Canterbury, holing up in Conquest House to strategise their attack, an act that led to the archbishop's canonisation.

The building itself is deceptive – it appears to be late Tudor or Jacobean, and its fascinating exterior includes a hanging panel showing one of the four knights, and dragon motifs keeping a watchful eye on proceedings. These are, of course, later additions, done in the 19th century, and the building has been described by some purists in architectural circles as 'phony'. Conquest House has recently housed a plastics-free wholefoods and vegetable shop, and one imagines Becket would approve of the shop's commitment to responsible living. It was sadly closed at printing, but when it opens again – and it surely will – be sure to take in the Norman undercroft, galleried hall and decorative 17th-century fireplace. Now that it is surrounded by the vibrant and most definitely safe area of King's Mile, the only crime now would be not to admire this architectural mishmash, the site of a murderous plot.

Address 17 Palace Street, CT1 2DZ | Getting there 10-minute walk from Canterbury West station; Canterbury West station car park | Hours Exterior unrestricted | Tip This street is no stranger to historical crime. The nearby Bell and Crown pub's landlord, William Madden, was summoned in the late 1800s for allowing prostitutes to drink longer in his house than considered reasonable.

15__ The Crooked House

How low can you go?

No, it's not your eyes. This 17th-century house is indeed skewed. A popular theory for its lop-sidedness was once that a giant leant on it, but the real culprit is of course more prosaic: unsuccessful adjustments to the large internal chimney. The chimney collapsed in the 1980s, but the building was saved thanks to intervention by the Canterbury Archaeological Trust and the council. Because of the damage suffered, a new front door had to be built with extremely skewed corners to fit the door frame. Although the interior isn't as eye-catching as the outside, the low ceilings and ancient beams are worth a look too. A brick cellar too dangerous for the public to visit is rumoured to be a cavernous delight.

The large windows are thought to have been installed to maximize light for the city's weavers who would have once worked here creating fine silks and cottons. These talented émigrés from Belgium (Walloons) and France (Huguenots) settled in Canterbury in the 17th century to escape religious persecution at home. Canterbury was especially popular due to the commercial pull of the river and closeness to London, until the easy availability of East Indian silks began to take its toll on business. Mechanisation became the final threat and by 1837 demand was in inexorable decline.

Murder, piety and medieval intrigue are words more usually applied to the history of Canterbury, but such lopsided houses add a splash of comedy.

This one's peculiarity lends itself perfectly to creative establishments, and in the past it has served as a gallery and an instrument shop. Now it's Catching Lives Bookshop, featuring a wide range of second-hand paperbacks. The stock is all donated and the shop is run entirely by volunteers, so its proceeds can go towards the homeless so make a visit if you can. Try not to tip over as you pass through the door!

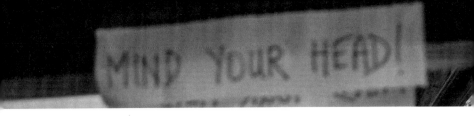

Address 28 Palace Street, CT1 2DZ, +44 (0)7899 458961, www.catchinglives.org/catching-lives-bookshop | Getting there 10-minute walk from Canterbury West station via St Peter's Street and the High Street before turning into Guildhall Street and then Palace Street; Canterbury West station car park | Hours Exterior unrestricted | Tip Crane your neck to make out the figure of a Native American at the apex of the building, created at a time when the new world was opening up.

16 Dane John's Mound
From burials to ... picnics

This grassy temple, crowned by something not unlike a historic telephone transmitter, overlooks and lends its name to the neat lawns and borders of the peaceful relaxation spot of Dane John Gardens. The mound though – resembling a grassy pyramid – hides a mountain of secrets. Once a burial mound, it alone remains from a group of four Romano-British burial mounds in the vicinity, dating from around the first or second century AD.

Dane John's Mound was elevated into the city's framework after the Battle of Hastings of 1066, when Canterbury surrendered to William the Conqueror, who established a defence here. It was a great site for a castle as it would have been protected by the remains of the Roman defensive wall and ramparts. It is thought that the motte (the fortification part of the structure at the top) was added later.

Canterbury's locals would cavort on the mound in the medieval period and would even lay their clothes out to dry or bleach on it as they relaxed in the gardens.

Its relative isolation later made it a natural home for the poor infected souls of the Black Death in 1630, who were left here to die in tents, and it has also been instrumental in the city's sewage system and rubbish management. At the end of the 17th century the site was used as a place for military executions, including those of deserters, and during World War II it became an ammunition depot. By the late 18th century, the gardens were revved up and the mound was made more accessible, with a spiral hedge-lined pathway. Climbing it is something of a test due to its steepness but is worth the effort for its views. The gardens are also filled with other things to see such as a peace pavement (see ch. 19) and a Grade II listed sundial, but it is the mound which takes you by surprise at the centre of this popular lunchtime spot, with many visitors unaware of its dark past.

Address CT1 2WR | **Getting there** 15-minute walk through city centre via Canterbury West station before turning right at Fenwick; limited parking | **Hours** Unrestricted | **Tip** In 2011, around 150 graves were found during an excavation in St Dunstan's Street, once a suburb of Roman Canterbury. The Roman road from Dover to London followed the line of St Dunstan's Street, and Roman finds at this site date from as early as the first century AD.

17 Double Sword Burial
Live by the sword, die by the sword

Excavations of Roman burials normally undercover pots and coins and maybe the odd piece of jewellery, yet a 1970s excavation in Canterbury revealed the skeletons of two men buried head to toe and lying on top of one another in a shallow pit, along with their swords – all very unusual.

Canterbury was known as *Durovernum Cantiacorum* in Roman times, and a series of ditches were also found at the excavation site suggesting there may have been a fort in the area between the middle and late first century AD, around which the later settlement grew. While the skeletons are not on display, the swords they were buried with are, and date the burials to the late second or third century AD. It is these rare artefacts which join the UK's only remaining *in situ* Roman pavement mosaics in a museum which brims with Roman life but here focusses on death.

The burial of these two individuals with their swords raises suspicions. The Roman army was strict about returning valuable weapons, so such *spatha* swords, used by every soldier in the Roman army, are rarely found in burials. Analysis indicates that these decayed swords' scabbards (blade covers) were created of wood, and that the shorter sword was made from iron strips forged together, while the longer sword had a central twisted bar. Despite their age, their length and sophisticated design mean they remain fearsome today. Part of their design success is down to their long 'tangs', the continuation of the metal from the blade into the (usually wooden, or bone) handle. The tang element gave soldiers a superior grip and prevented the sword from snapping. Yet such dangerous weaponry was not enough to protect these unfortunate two. Whether it was a murder or a suicide pact, or even death by disease, remains unknown. All we do know is that for some, death in Roman times truly was a double-edged sword.

Address Canterbury Roman Museum, Butchery Lane, CT1 2JR, +44 (0)1227 785575, www.canterburymuseums.co.uk/romanmuseum | **Getting there** 10-minute walk via Canterbury West station onto Station Road and via the High Street; Queningate car park | **Hours** Daily 10am–5pm | **Tip** You will be able to spy Roman remnants such as red tiles all over the city, with St Martin's Church and Queningate being notable examples. Also, a Roman road, Watling Street, passed through Canterbury linking it to the Kentish ports of Dubris (Dover) and Rutupiae (Richborough).

18 East Train Station
A signal of more romantic times

With a glorious farmers' market making use of its former goods
shed (see ch. 22) and the fast trains to St Pancras whizzing through,
Canterbury West station attracts attention and welcomes Londoners seeking a break. But its easterly counterpart also has many stories to tell, and the views of the city as you arrive from London are
stunning.

One of its most noted claims to fame is its link to world-famous
mystery maestro Arthur Conan Doyle. In his collection of short story
The Memoirs of Sherlock Holmes, Holmes and Watson are described as
stealing away from arch-enemy Professor Moriarty in a train station
in Canterbury. The pages indicate that the pair were making their
way to catch up with a boat for the Continental Express to London
Victoria, so this would have been the station Conan Doyle described.
Nowadays, the station is more likely to serve the workers based in
nearby Kentish towns such as Sittingbourne and Chatham rather
than metropolitan Victorian sleuths.

The station also has a design element to note. Look a little further
next time you buy a ticket, and you will find an elevated wooden signal box on stilts, painted pale green and cream. The steel substructure
raises it one extra storey, enabling signalmen to see over the station
roof to the far side of the station. It is the only surviving example of
the South Eastern and Chatham Railway's own distinctive design,
used between 1899 and 1921. Opened circa 1911, this signal box
was given a Grade II listed building status in 2013, two years after
its functional century of life came to an end. Demolishment had
loomed, but local conservation efforts saved it at the very last minute.
Even though this signal box is no longer in practical use, its charm-
ing design evoking the romance of early train travel will ensure that
Canterbury East station will always be part of the beautiful view for
arrivals and departures.

Address Station Road East, CT1 2RB | **Getting there** There are regular trains to Canterbury East station from stations all over Kent and from London; parking on site | **Hours** Check with station staff if you need to buy a ticket to view the signal box | **Tip** Herne Bay station, which opened in 1861, featured briefly in an episode of the BBC comedy *Some Mothers Do Mothers Do 'Ave 'Em.*

19 European Peace Pavement

An artistic response to peace

Blinking at you on a sunny day is an unusual collection of public art, speaking quietly of unification and reconciliation. Lifting the spirits and making a welcome change from solemn war memorials are 16 individual stones made by artists set amongst a plain, unworked York paving stone.

In place since 1993, the Peace Pavement was developed when artists from 16 European cities including Canterbury, all of which had been bombed during the 20th century, were asked to create their own response to peace both as individuals and as artists. This artistic project celebrated the opening up of Europe, offering a new and exciting prospect for Eastern European artists who travelled from places such as St Petersburg and Vladimir. They worked in an old garage in Pound Lane, with some of the images being carved into the stone and some sandblasted. A place of wartime activity, Dane John Park was chosen, to showcase the work celebrating the opening of European borders. Landscaping was designed around the pavement and benches installed creating a peaceful and contemplative space just off the busy city centre. In fractured times it is a welcoming reminder of the sanctity of peace. Unfortunately suffering its own damage in the past years, it has been refurbished and cleaned earlier this decade to make it (hopefully) vandal-proof. The public art project has also influenced other artworks such as Martin John Callanan's sobering *Wars During My Lifetime*.

The Peace Pavement talks of links and ties with our overseas neighbours – once our enemies, and despite recent political upheaval, now our friends. It's interesting to note that the predominant feature of the park is a Romano-British burial mound from the 1st or 2nd century AD (see ch. 16). Perhaps climb to the top and survey your surroundings, considering the weight of history, and how much of it has been spent in war and conquest.

Address Dane John Gardens, CT1 2QX, www.explorekent.org | Getting there 15-minute walk from Canterbury West station through city centre before turning right at Fenwick; Whitefriars car park | Hours Unrestricted | Tip Although it is a replica, the elegant Victorian-style bandstand in the park is worth a look. If you're visiting in the summer, there may be a concert on.

20__Fordwich

Spend more than a penny in this well-heeled town

Tiny Fordwich is one of a handful of towns in Britain competing to be the smallest. Bucolic and hidden away, whether it is the smallest is debatable, but it must be one of the prettiest. Fine houses, yew trees and an oast house all contribute to its Kentish charm and the tidal Stour cradles it. The village emerged from a Roman settlement in the first century and its ancient buildings are a highpoint.

The miniature Town Hall dates back to circa 1544 and is a must-visit. With its pretty red-and-black design it makes for an unusual wedding venue. Less happily, it incorporates one door to the old prison. For crimes such as poaching the plump Fordwich trout, you would have been locked in this dank space which last held prisoners in 1885. In the Hall's upstairs jury room, jurors deliberated for many hours on a case and would not be allowed outside until they had made their decision, so a strategic hole for them to relieve themselves is still visible. If you were found guilty of gossip you would be dunked in the river. The ducking stool displayed is a replica of one first used in 1465.

Today, Fordwich is more inclined to dunk you in local sparkling white wine. The Fordwich Arms opposite the Town Hall is a much-celebrated draw, offering innovative cooking to savour in an oak-panelled dining room. Just around the corner is another must-visit in Fordwich – the shingle church of St Mary's, England's smallest town church. Inside it is home to a strange carved stone dating from around 1100 believed to be a shrine made for the body parts – or relics – of a saint. The remains are thought to be of St Augustine of Canterbury who popularized Christianity in England (see ch. 43). If you want to stay in Fordwich then you could take up the church's scheme of champing – camping in the church. It's a nicer place to stay than the tiny prison, and they let you out in the morning.

Address CT2 0BY | Getting there Bus from Canterbury or Thanet to Fordwich Road, then an 8-minute walk over two river bridges, bearing left at the George and Dragon pub onto King Street; Sturry Road Park and Ride parking | Hours Town Hall: May–Sep Sun 1.30–4pm (group visits year-round, call +44 (0)1227 711950) | Tip There are public footpaths leading from Fordwich to the varied wildlife of Westbere Lakes. Follow the cow parsley and hawthorn of the Stour on the north bank until you reach the lakes; the path then heads towards the peaceful village of Westbere itself.

21__Gas Street Oast House

From house of hops to house and home?

A rare example of an agricultural building in Canterbury, this mid-19th-century, brick 'oast' house is found within the city walls near the ruins of the Norman castle. Although derelict and covered with graffiti, this building is an interesting version of one of Kent's most enduring symbols. The oasts of Kent were more commonly conical in shape, so this one is unusual for being square. Grade II listed with a distinctive hipped roof, it is thought to have replaced an original timber version.

Called oast houses in Kent, these buildings are known as hop kilns elsewhere in England. Wherever they were to be found, whatever they were called, they were key to the local brewery trade. Fresh hops would be gathered in the 'stowage' of the oast house before being placed in the oast to be dried via a wood or charcoal fire. Heat would travel up through the hops and escape through a revolving chimney cowl. Once dry, the hops would be collected by the brewery.

As Kent's brewing industry flourished from the 16th century onward, merry locals would have imbibed ale in their favourite inns at Beer Cart Lane and nearby Stour Street (see ch. 49) and Londoners drank the fruits of Kentish crops enthusiastically too. Frequently grown on farms but also found wild in hedgerows, these green flowers brought a level of prosperity that had *Robinson Crusoe* author Daniel Defoe commenting in 1724 that, 'so that now they may say without boasting, there is at Canterbury the greatest plantation of hops in the whole island'.

Reliable details of this oast house's early history are scant. Its most recent use was as a museum building in the 1980s. Many of Kent's oast houses have been adapted for residential use, and it looks like this one may be taken down the same route. For a look at the conical types adorning Kent's tourist brochures, make your way to Wickhambreaux (see ch. 56) or Fordwich (see ch. 20).

Address CT1 2PR | Getting there 10-minute walk from Canterbury East station via Pin Hill and Castle Street; Castle Street car park | Hours Exterior unrestricted | Tip Established in 1970, Gibson's Farm Shop found in Wingham, outside Canterbury, stocks ale crafted by locally based brewers including Canterbury Ales, some of which are named after Chaucer's characters.

22___The Goods Shed

Windows on the prize produce of Kent

A formerly derelict Victorian railway goods shed a few steps away from Canterbury West station has been the perfect home for the country's first full-time farmer's market since 2002. Glossy fish join purple sprouting broccoli and rhubarb-infused preserves alongside the largest number of British bottled beers in the southeast of England. Jolly butchers advise on how to get to grips with whole local carcasses for most of us now only familiar with supermarket cuts; elsewhere the best of the vegetable farms of East Kent is on offer. You could easily while away an hour or two just browsing produce not only from Canterbury and its surrounding areas, but also from overseas. Charcuterie, ham and honey as well as a range of cheeses are imported from the Basque country and Provence. But the bounty of Kent remains unmatched, and The Goods Shed Restaurant is the place to sample it. You may have succumbed to a tasting menu before, but have you ever indulged in a banquet? Have one fit for King Ethelbert here. Swoon as waiters bring plates of traditional game doused with juniper and brandy. Smoked eels blush with scarlet beetroot and cobnuts are crushed into sauce and paired with ice-cream. Finish with botanically inspired cocktails, and as you savour each mouthful listen to the hum of the market as talented gourmets offer their wares to curious gastronomes.

And in a county bursting with milk, cream and butter, make sure to try the local cheeses such as Canterbury Goat and Canterbury Cobble. Ashmore cheese stands out for its Cheddar-like flavour and versatility, and you'll find it served up in a rarebit, moulded into croquettes or just proudly paired with other local cheeses in the poshest of restaurants as well as the most ancient and homely of inns.

An elegant Victorian structure, a fine local brew, a bite of punchy Ashmore … Culinary pilgrims have never had it so good.

CALABRIAN LEMON
EXTRA VIRGIN OLIVE OIL
...s delicious oil is from
...thern Italy. A wonderful
...g for salads & fish dishes

...95 500ml: 9.95 1litre: 17.00

ORGANIC BALSAMIC VINEGAR
This mature balsamic is a great
everyday vinegar. It is perfect for
dipping or a salad dressing. Unlike
many balsamics, this is entirely natural
& contains no colour or flavour enhancers.

250ml: 6.50 500ml: 10.00 1litre: 18.00

Address Station Road West, CT2 8AN, +44 (0)1227 459153, www.thegoodsshed.co.uk |
Getting there Turn left out of Canterbury West station and you're there; Canterbury West
station car park | Hours Market: Tue–Sat 9am–7pm (winter 6pm), Sun 10am–4pm;
restaurant: Mon–Fri noon–2.30pm & 5.30–9.30pm, Sat 8–10.30am, noon–3pm,
5.30–9.30pm, Sun 9–10.30am & noon–3pm | Tip Want to be an environmental star as
you sample Kent's fine produce? Head to Lower Hardres Farm Shop to pick your own
berries in the summer (www.lowerhardresfarmshop.co.uk).

23__Greyfriars Chapel

England's first Franciscan house

Walk along a thin sliver of the Stour and a strip of pastel wildflowers to reach the Greyfriars, the first Franciscan house in England, dating back to the 13th century.

The friars took the anti-materialistic values of simplicity and piety of reformed playboy St Francis of Assisi to heart at a time when senior ecclesiastical figures bathed in luxury. The first barefooted Grey Friars in Kent aroused suspicion and fear, but they soon won locals over with their sincerity and commitment to a humble life. Many Franciscan buildings in England have now disappeared, so it is a thing of some wonder to see this one, with its flint walls and elegant chancel, in good condition.

The Black Death took two-thirds of the friars in 1348, and during the peasants' revolt of 1381, Jack Straw, one of the movement's leaders, called for the destruction of the whole church – except the Franciscans. When the friars were in this house it was much coveted for its location, so it's no surprise that after the 16th-century Dissolution of the Monasteries it was bought and used as a private residence, before being occupied by Huguenot refugees escaping an unsafe France in 1683. Graffiti on the studded door of the of the ground floor indicated it was probably used as a lock-up for the Bridewell (prison) in the Poor Priests' Hospital in the 19th century. During World War I, Belgian refugees benefitted from its shelter.

These days it has reverted to its original use as a place of worship, and you may even see some cloaked friars on your visit. Upstairs has been furnished as a chapel and vestry, and if you time it right (Wednesdays at 12.30pm) you will be able to attend a service, gaining a glimpse of this part of history, and insight into an order now becoming something of a rarity. Having gained fame as the first of its kind in the country, hopefully it will not end up as one of its last. And the adjacent gardens are a peaceful oasis.

Address 25 High Street, CT1 2BD | Getting there 12-minute walk from Canterbury West station via St Peter's Lane; Rosemary Lane car park | Hours Daily 2–4pm, exterior unrestricted | Tip Funky Monks on St Peter's Street is a paean to vintage fashion specialising in garments from the 1960s to the 1980s with many unique items. You might even find a habit.

24__House of Correction
Crime can pay at this glorious building

If you are ever unlucky or nefarious enough to find yourself behind bars, then this would be the sort of place to go. Surrounded by bright flowers and in a Grade II listed building, this would be internment at its finest. Apart from the massive wrought-iron entrance and the lettering above it, there is not much to suggest that this establishment was ever a gaol. Still, the sinister beauty of the building isn't lost on location hunters, and it has been used as a backdrop for the BBC drama *Capture*. Closed in 2013, it is now being converted into a wing of Canterbury Christ Church University.

Jane Austen is said to have visited, most probably to accompany her brother Edward, who was a visiting magistrate at the time. But the most high-profile inmates were undoubtedly the notorious Kray brothers, twin gangsters down from London for an unforgettable stop on their tour of the country's prisons including Maidstone prison.

Before being a hold-up centre for London's finest criminal aristocracy, the prison was somewhat progressive with a treadmill installed not just for punishment but for an actual useful purpose which was to pump water (for nine-hour stints) to nearby Kent and Canterbury Hospital. But by the 1940s the rising prison populations led to over-crowding, tension and violence. The prison was also late to offer education for inmates until a new block was established in the 1970s. By the 1990s a critical inspection report deemed the place too small for its purpose and it found a new role as the first non-military prison in the UK to hold only foreign national prisoners before shutting its doors and abandoning its peeling walls. It is not open to the public but who wants to eat porridge every day amongst the 20-foot prison walls that hold stories of hardship and crime anyway – even if your breakfast companions were once more interesting than your average con.

Address North Holmes Road, CT1 1QU, +44 (0)1227 767700, www.canterbury.ac.uk/about-us/estate-master-plan/prison-conversion | Getting there 10-minute walk from Canterbury East station via Lady Wootton's Green and Monastery Street; limited parking on site | Hours Exterior unrestricted, no public entry | Tip One Pound Lane dates back to 1829 and was a prison extension before turning into a police station. Now an Instagram-friendly bar and kitchen, it does a nice line in incarceration-themed cocktails (www.onepoundlane.co.uk).

25 __ K & Canterbury Hospital
A design for life

In 1937, health and style joined forces in Canterbury for a brave new look to the city's vernacular. From outside you can admire the chunky, unmistakably Art Deco clock so beloved by locals that there was even a spirited campaign to save it from demolition.

Cinemas and hotels fell under the spell of the angular lines and geometric shapes that characterised the distinctive Art Deco architecture and design movement of the 1920s and 1930s. Municipal buildings adopted the look less often, due to post-World War I austerity. You can see a bit of Art Deco style in Canterbury in the windows in the ladies' toilets of the Curzon cinema (see ch. 54), at The Peter Cushing Wetherspoon's in Whitstable and even in the pastiche style of Tiny Tim's Tearoom on St Margaret's Street. There are also several Art Deco residences in Herne Bay and Whitstable, but generally speaking, this part of the world was lightly touched by the movement. This reinforced-concrete hospital is one of the few examples of Art Deco architecture in Canterbury, although later architectural additions have blurred the original vision. Designed by Kent-based Cecil Burns in 1935, it was opened by the Duke of Kent. Other Art Deco stylings are the graceful Sun Balcony (solarium), now a ward. These were not unusual in hospitals of an era when sunlight and fresh air were considered a cure for many ills. Also, of note are the stark, elongated curve and elegant handrails of the main staircase.

The original Kent and Canterbury hospital was built on three acres of former abbey land in Longport in 1793, and no longer exists. During World War II, the modern hospital was an emergency rest centre for city residents. Until 1948, when it became part of the National Health Service, it was a voluntary hospital, financed by charitable contributions. This proudly 20th-century hospital offers a view of architecture from a period rarely witnessed in the city.

Address Ethelbert Road, CT1 3NG, +44 (0)1227 766877, www.ekhuft.nhs.uk/patients-and-visitors/kent-and-canterbury-hospital | **Getting there** Bus 25, 25a directly from the main bus depot; parking on site | **Hours** Exterior unrestricted | **Tip** Art Deco's predecessor, swirly Art Nouveau, lit up the first-floor windows of now empty chain store Debenhams in Guildhall Street and a stained-glass window in St Dunstan's Church.

26___Kentish Stour

Not just a pretty place

In Roman and medieval times this river was not just a watery feature of Canterbury's beauty, but a major transport route. It connected with the nearby town of Fordwich via its busy, ancient port, through which the Caen stone that made up the cathedral was hauled. Much later, activities such as corn milling, paper making and electricity generation all buzzed along, supporting the city and contributing to its wealth.

Today, much of the action happens under the water. Bream, brown trout and European eels – which once formed the basis of many medieval treats – swim amongst the chalkiness. The second-longest river in Kent, it is lined with knobbly shrubs and graceful willows. Vibrant kingfishers swoop down to the warm waters, but they are not easy to spot. You might be even luckier and spot the emblem of English rivers, the vole.

The Stour also played a key role in the spread of Christianity. The riverside is dotted with historic inns for thirsty pilgrims, and a Franciscan island and chapel lie between its banks. As well as the pious, its teeming waters have also attracted anglers. It is reputed that the freedom to fish here within the city dates back to an edict issued by King Canute. Another feature is the ducking stool just visible from the gabled Old Weaver's House in the High Street and from ASK restaurant.

Crowds gawp, but it is not an accurate presentation of the past, as ducking stools of this kind would often have been on wheels and placed outside a 'scold's' home to ignite shame rather than punish. Medieval society placed great worth on what they deemed acceptable behaviour and the (mainly) women who were targeted by the stool's presence would have been mortified enough to adapt their behaviour to avoid the drastic step of an unceremonious dunking. But from any vantage point, the Stour's watery charms are much loved.

Address The best site for the ducking stool is ASK restaurant, The Kings Bridge, 24 High Street, CT1 2AY | Getting there 8-minute walk from Canterbury West station; Canterbury West station car park | Hours Unrestricted | Tip Seeking adventure? You can kayak or canoe these waters, and if you have the stamina, you can make it all the way to beautiful Grove Ferry.

27 — Lady Wootton's Green

For richer, for poorer

Long before this pocket of green belonged to the Lady Wootton of its name, it felt the feet of Queen Bertha, Princess of the Franks, wife of King Ethelbert (see ch. 43) as she made her way along her devotional route (see ch. 39) towards St Martin's Church (see ch. 12) in the late 6th century. Once St Augustine's Abbey was established, the green became part of a ceremonial route between the city and the abbey. From the 12th century, it was where the abbey's almonry handed out donations for the poor.

After the dissolution of the monasteries in 1539, it formed part of Henry VIII's extensive property portfolio, and his fourth wife, Anne of Cleves, stayed in the former abbot's lodging at the end of that year, on her way to meet her husband-to-be. The green wouldn't have been green at all then, but rather a sort of builders' yard, where various types of stone and slate were available while the repurposing of the buildings took place. In 1612, Queen Mary leased the palace to Edward Lord Wootton. Lady Wootton proved to be rather land-hungry, and the estate incurred strict financial penalties for restricting access to the king's highway and the common watercourse.

After Lady Wootton's death in 1659, lessees of the property continued to encroach upon the green, largely 'waste' land, fit for grazing rather than farming. In the Victorian era, artisan and working-class families made the area around the green their home. Many of the medieval buildings surrounding it were destroyed in World War II. Fyndon Gate suffered Blitz damage, but careful restoration means that the grand and incredibly detailed 14th-century archway is impossible to miss. Named after Abbott Fyndon, who commissioned an ambitious building programme to update St Augustine's, the gate was part of a brewery in the 1820s, but is now part of the King's School, the oldest independent school in Britain. Orlando Bloom is an alumnus.

Address CT1 1NG | Getting there 12-minute walk from Canterbury East direction following the Broadgate route; Queningate car park | Hours Unrestricted access; Fyndon Gate exterior access only | Tip A wing of the King's School is located on another former almonry. Mint Yard's name reflects the brief 16th-century period when coins were minted for the crown here. No entry but you can view the decorative Tudor brickwork.

28 London Plane Tree

Try tying a yellow ribbon round this!

Children laugh at it, lovers smooch under it, the rest of us gawp at it. Not every city tree can claim to turn heads, but the London plane tree of Westgate Gardens deserves a double take. With its massive, gnarled trunk and unwieldy branches, it looks like something out of a Tim Burton movie. One of several in the city, including the one near the castle, this tree is by far the most impressive. Its bulbous trunk dominates the surroundings, and the other trees cower in its shadow. When nature flourishes in the city it is always cheering. The fact that this *jolie-laide* specimen is so unusual makes it all the more special.

It was first thought of as an Oriental plane tree, but this is now considered contentious; the Natural History Museum are of the opinion that it is a type of London plane. Thought to have been planted in the 19th century it would have most probably taken root to combat the effects of pollution and enhance public health. But back to today, this London plane has evolved in a way that differentiates itself from its contemporaries. According to some reports, it swallowed up the circular seat that once surrounded it sometime at the turn of the last century. But how did it get its bizarre shape? The swollen trunk is thought to be the result of a viral infection, but this has been debated. Is its peculiar look a by-product of ill health?

Nature cannot speak but what we do know is that this tree is one of the oldest of its kind in the county. It is also probably the tree with the widest girth in the city and is thought to be two centuries into its life. Though, of course, no one will be chopping this monster down and counting its rings although another historic tree in the city has been cut down due to its pavement location. Hopefully, the green surroundings of this specimen will ensure its continuing longevity. The Baobab trees, as they are also known, because they share similar qualities with trees of the same name in Africa, are just another part of this city's enduring mystery. Maybe one day the truth will out.

Address Westgate Gardens, St Peter's Street, CT1 2BQ | Getting there 5-minute walk from Canterbury West station; Canterbury West station car park | Hours Daily 9am – 6pm | Tip The nearby Tower House is an elegant, architecturally diverse structure dating back to the Victorian era, now a popular wedding venue (www.towerhousecanterbury.co.uk).

29 — Longmarket
Canterbury scene and heard

In the brutal Baedeker raids of 1942, Longmarket and its medieval architecture took a mighty hit. The devastation gave the city an unexpected chance to discover more about the area and fuelled significant archaeological excavations over the decades. Finds included part of a Roman townhouse with an elaborate mosaic corridor, later absorbed into the Roman museum (see ch. 17). Post-1990 evidence of rubbish tips dating from the 12th century onwards was also discovered.

Within the city centre and close to the cathedral, Longmarket was revealed to have housed Canterbury's wealthy and influential citizens including Theoric the Goldsmith, mentioned in documents dating back to 1180. According to William Urry, an expert on medieval Canterbury, he was one of the 'great men' of the city, setting up a Royal Exchange being just one of his many achievements. Others were not so influential and died without praise or even a suitable burial, as evidenced by the remains of a medieval man in his 20s blighted by dental abnormalities. The lack of ceremony in his burial suggests foul play.

Commercial buildings of the late 20th and early 21st centuries respect Longmarket's rich history. The shopping development was constructed in a continuous line to follow the historic buildings of the south-eastern stretch of narrow Butchery Lane. Look up to take in the steeply pitched roofs, clay tiles and gables of old, and you can almost hear the excited babble of the pilgrims.

Musicians were also drawn to the Longmarket and its square, and the bands that made up the Canterbury scene (see ch. 54) pitched up around here in the 1960s and 1970s. A contemporary band that has made a successful leap from city busking to national popularity is CoCo and the Butterfields, who launched CoCo TV during the coronavirus pandemic to continue entertaining their fans when they were unable to tour.

Address CT1 2JS | **Getting there** 12-minute walk from Canterbury West station through the High Street and Rose Lane; Queningate car park | **Hours** Unrestricted | **Tip** Go underground without the need of a digger. Café Mauresque on Butchery Lane combines plates of north African and Spanish food with a cosy ambience in its underground level full of jewelled cushions and flickering tealights (www.cafemauresque.co.uk).

30__Marks & Spencer
A beautiful survivor

The familiar sight of the beloved chain rarely receives much attention from the likes of the glossy architectural magazines or even from its many shoppers who scramble in for lunch. Marks & Spencer Canterbury is just a place to buy socks, isn't it? Well, no. You can consider this store, which dates back to the 1930s, as a must see in a city crammed full of buildings to note.

During World War II, the store narrowly avoided being destroyed by the Baedeker raid of 1942, which took down most of the neighbouring properties. With true plucky spirit, the shop was cleaned up and reopened a few days after the attack thanks to the watchman's capable assistance in hosing down the flames. The store also became something of a hero itself when parts of it were used by the Ministry of Food during the conflict – apt when you consider the store's famous sandwiches and cakes. As the only retail place in St George's Street to survive the raid, this must be down to a divine nod to both its peerless food and architectural glory.

Graceful and sweeping, its façade is considered to be one of the most stylish of the stores built during the period. For others with similar appeal, you will need to head far away in the direction of Winchester or Peterborough. Over the decades, the store has undergone various extensions and revisions, but the front reveals the essence of its history. Look up from the mannequins towards the ornately carved swags of leaves and fruit.

With many Marks & Spencer stores now closing, it would be a shame not just for hungry lunchers, but anyone interested in the city's history too if it were to be closed or, heaven forbid, modernized out of recognition. Canterbury stores such as Nasons and Ricemans have fallen by the wayside. Marks & Spencer Canterbury has outlived them all and even survived the Nazis. But can it survive the internet?

Address 4 St George's Street, CT1 2SR, +44 (0)1227 462281, www.whitesfriars.co.uk/shopping/marks-spencer | Getting there 15-minute walk from Canterbury West station via St Peter's Street and then the High Street; Whitefriars car park | Hours Exterior unrestricted | Tip Vic Kimpton Menswear at Mortimer Street in Herne Bay is a rare example of a traditional gentlemen's outfitters helmed by the knowledgeable Vic in a tiny but crammed space.

31 Marlowe Statue

Spare your blushes

Standing near the theatre that bears his name, this 19th-century memorial to Christopher Marlowe has been through almost as much drama as the writer's famed works. Financial pressures, several relocations, World War II damage and later vandalism have all taken their toll on Kitty Marlowe (as she is referred to by locals – the playwright was known as Kit). It was not until the 1990s that Sir Ian McKellen rededicated it in its present location outside the Marlowe Theatre.

Designed by sculptor Onslow Ford in bronze, the semi-nude statue was considered saucy at first. Thought especially risqué for her first site at the Buttermarket (see ch. 4) in the shadow of the holy folk at the cathedral, Kitty was relocated to Dane John Gardens. She graces a pedestal featuring a Marlovian character on each of the four sides. The city's dramatic leanings during Marlowe's times were rich, and plays would have been performed in courtyards, inns and private houses.

You'll find Christopher Marlowe's name added to many of the city's other landmarks. The Renaissance writer was born in the city to a local shoemaker and was educated here. His life was mired in intrigue and gossip, including speculation that he was variously a spy, a homosexual and an atheist who told jokes about the Bible – not wise for the time. Perhaps the most celebrated rumour surrounding him is that he was responsible for Shakespeare's works. It's not a rumour that he was a tempestuous type, though. He once attacked a lute player, William Corkine, with a staff and dagger, at Mercery Lane. Both parties tried to file a case for assault. He was eventually killed, allegedly over a disputed bill in a London tavern, but we'll never know the true motivation behind his murder. The brawling Marlowe certainly does not live up to the idea that poets are gentle creatures, despite the delicacy of this statue.

Address The Friars, CT1 2AS | Getting there 10-minute walk from either railway station; several car parks nearby including Miller's Field and Pound Lane | Hours Unrestricted | Tip Located in a wonderful 12th-century building on Stour Street, The Marlowe Kit offers new ways to learn about Canterbury's rich literary heritage and engage in its future (www.marlowetheatre.com/about/what-we-do/the-marlowe-kit).

32 Marlowe Theatre
All the city's a stage

Canterbury loves a bit of drama, and 16 theatres have thrilled audiences in the city over the years. The remains of a Roman amphitheatre lie underneath the cellars of St Margaret's Street and Tudor theatre took place in local inns. The city's first theatre impresario combined her acting background with uncanny business acumen in the late 18th century when Mrs Sarah Baker operated the Buttermarket House plus many other theatres in Kent. Little of these entertaining establishments is now on show.

Much of today's drama takes place in the Marlowe Theatre, which owes its name to Canterbury's famed dramatist. It is in fact the city's third, the first Marlowe Theatre having stood where the Marlowe / Whitefriars Arcade (see ch. 55) is now. The second evolved from the converted 1930s cinema, The Friars, which was demolished in 2009. It was replaced by the shimmering, present-day Marlowe Theatre in 2011, to the tune of £26 million.

The story of this building, including its eight-metre-high colonnade in white cast Dolomite stone and expansive fly stage (where much of the staging is planned), reveals its own dramatic narrative. Necessary archaeological work to the west of the theatre revealed a Roman townhouse with five rooms suggesting high status. However, the presence of the nearby Stour impacted the dig, and three of the rooms were below water level, with diggers working in damp conditions. Heating systems were discovered, as were clay floors mainly painted in red, white and black. Several vast medieval pits were also discovered; they normally would have stored household rubbish. Lines of preserved timber revetments, designed to lessen the ingress of the Stour, were also uncovered.

Few clues to the site's watery past are evident now, although if you fancy dazzling views of the city, today's towering Marlowe Theatre is a modern marvel.

Address The Friars, CT1 2AS, +44 (0)1227 787787, www.marlowetheatre.com | Getting there 8-minute walk from Canterbury West station past Westgate Towers and St Peter's Street before turning left down St Peter's Lane; St Radigund's car park | Hours Exterior unrestricted; see website for performances | Tip Kent-born sculptor Rick Kirby's gigantic *Bulkhead* mask is located nearby with its expressive face conveying the essence of drama.

33 Masonic Aprons

A rare insight into the shadowy world

Nowadays associated with secrecy and controversy, Freemasonry emerged from the practice of stonemasonry. Workers would greet each other with a particular handshake in order to cement their credibility. These stonemasons were thought to be responsible for some of the most intricate buildings in the country, including Canterbury's cathedral and castle. Key to the stonemason was the protective apron, and several can be viewed here, including blue-and-white one. Masonic aprons vary with the wearer's rank within the organisation. However, admiring such a garment provokes a useful indicator of the standard masonic dress as the majority of aprons are comprised of a shade of blue and white. Other versions are also on display with the oldest dating back to 1730.

Aprons have been a symbolic accessory for centuries, in civilizations as disparate as China, Central America and Scotland. The earliest ceremonial apron dates back to 2200 BC when the king of Palestine used a white lambskin. Lambskin became the material of choice for the Freemasons within their own costume. The Kent Museum of Freemasonry, a free display of the country's largest collection of Freemasonry artefacts outside London, is staffed by perhaps the friendliest volunteers you could ever hope to meet. This is the place to look as long as you like at the Mason's uniform, as gaining access to a Masonic temple is not as simple. There are national variations on the apron but this one is imbued with the spirit of the English Freemason. Its pale blue colour reflects the pillars of education, monarchy and religion which are respectively Oxford University, Parliament and the cloak of the Virgin Mary. These establishment figures are all associated with blue. The apron is just one of many artefacts in this museum which provide a view into this mysterious world, where the practices within the organisation remain opaque.

Address 66 St Peter's Place, CT1 2DA, +44 (0)1227 785625,
www.kentmuseumoffreemasonry.org.uk | **Getting there** 5-minute walk from Canterbury
West station turning left down Station Road and past Westgate Gardens; Canterbury
Pound Lane car park | **Hours** Daily 10am – 4pm | **Tip** In 1818, the Ancient Order of
Foresters, an early financial organisation, bought what is now Whitstable Community
Museum & Gallery and their inscription is clearly visible over the door.

34_Medieval Fish Market Building

Just in time for dinner

Since the 14th century, Canterbury's fish markets have been authorised on several different sites around the town, including the High Street and Burgate. The medieval market sites and buildings that once traded in cattle, corn, butter and reeds have now all been lost, so treasure this one. The site dates back to 1480 when two tonnes of pale grey Folkestone Stone were laid down to create a paved market area. Fish was central to the medieval diet, as it observed religious convention and meat was banned three days a week. Salted herrings from Whitstable's coasts formed a key part of the local menu and there's even a window in the cathedral depicting a biblical catch.

This grand building in St Margaret's Street was designed by city surveyor Jesse White in 1788. It took over 30 long years to get it approved and financed before finally being built in 1822, beating out the lengthy wrangling of the revamp of St George's and its surrounding area (see ch. 44) in the 1940s and 1950s. The wait was worth it though. Much of the building's grandeur is owed to its Greek Revival influences. This architectural movement flourished at the end of the 18th century, and the Fish Market building distinguishes itself as a rare surviving example in Canterbury. Built in a low and compressed form, a popular feature of Greek Revival, its pitched 'pediment' (triangle above) is another giveaway, as are the 'fluted' Doric columns – the flutes are the grooves running down the columns. Also check out the iron work on the rear windows.

Further examples of Greek Revival are found at Longport Sessions House and Canterbury West station, which Karl Marx dismissed as 'dismal and dry … there is no trace of poetry about it'. Marx visited in 1866 and was so unimpressed by Canterbury as a whole that he 'happily' neglected to visit the cathedral.

Address 29A St Margaret's Street, CT1 2TG | **Getting there** 12-minute walk from Canterbury West station via St Peter's Street and High Street then turning left at St Margaret's Street; Whitefriars car park | **Hours** Exterior unrestricted | **Tip** For more fishy business, visit the Red Shelter at the western end of Herne Bay, standing out amongst the pastel beach huts. Formed in 1904, the Heron Angling Society has been welcoming anglers to this distinctive building since 1964.

35_Oddfellows Hall

Friendship, love and truth

Links to today's Oddfellows and its fraternal society ethos can be traced as far back as to the banding together of the Israelites exiled from Babylon in 587 BC. Today, their reach is global. Their arrival in England came when the ancient English Trade Guilds began to decline in the early part of the 18th century and the Oddfellows' philosophy of friendship and support proved attractive for many craftsmen. Yet by the late 18th century, the English authorities eyed the French revolution with fear, and the foreign-born Oddfellows organisation aroused suspicion. The society was deemed illegal and driven underground. Members carried on, using passwords and signs to organise secret Branch meetings.

The illegal status was overturned 1851 and even King William IV joined, becoming a lifelong member. By 1898 women were included too. The Oddfellows began to emerge as the largest and richest friendly society in the world. As modern society and industry evolved, employees (and their families) facing occupational hazards relating to heavy industry were protected by Oddfellows' membership against illness, injury or death at a time when there was no welfare state. And Lodges often included a surgeon right up until the National Health Service was introduced in 1948.

The Canterbury Lodge is a Grade II listed building dating back to 1810 and is the oldest Lodge in Kent. Its distinct white exterior is an unusual contrast to Canterbury's more familiar colours of honey and slate. The sash windows add character. Look upwards for the sign featuring the Oddfellows' Three Links symbol. This stands for Friendship, Love & Truth – the organisation's motto. Signs and symbols were important for early Oddfellows due to widespread illiteracy, and they proved essential for communication. Today the society raises funds for charity, offers friendship and sells financial products.

Address 5 Orange Street, CT1 2JA | Getting there 12-minute walk from Canterbury West station towards St Peter's Street, turning right into Best Lane then right again into Orange Street; Queningate car park | Hours Exterior unrestricted | Tip To gain an idea of the architectural style of the Canterbury Lodge and sip a French martini at the same time, then step next door into Bramley's which is part of their original building and features vintage sewing machines and antique books.

36 Old Dover Road

Spy Ian Fleming's inspiration

Author Ian Fleming often took inspiration from the world around him. And it is here at Canterbury's busy Old Dover Road where his legendary spy tore through the outskirts of town during the car chase featured in his 1955 novel, *Moonraker*. Fleming wrote, 'Bond did a racing change and swung the big car left at the Charing Fork, preferring the clear road by Chilham and Canterbury … Bond took the short cut out of Canterbury by the Old Dover Road …'

The 007 bus route that navigated this road is thought to have inspired the spy's infamous code name. The 007 service continues today, though it is now managed by National Express.

It is still possible to travel the Old Dover Road on a journey through some of Ian Fleming's favourite local areas around Canterbury and beyond. One such place is the writer's coastal cottage at St Margaret's near Dover. Also on the Bond map is the city suburb of Bekesbourne, where Fleming and his wife Ann moved in 1957. Their 18th-century, eight-bedroom house went under the title of the 'Old Palace'. And locals referred to the author as 'Commander' because of his clandestine wartime activities.

A small settlement south of Canterbury, approached from the A2 at Bridge, holds one of the clues to James Bond's early upbringing. The glamorous spy lived with his aunt in Pett Bottom, near the Duck Inn, which was one of Fleming's favourite pubs and where it is claimed he wrote, *You Only Live Twice*. When James Bond apparently dies, his boss, the mysterious 'M', writes an obituary in *The Times*, in which he mentions the historic pub.

Driving within the speed limit, the journey to Dover today will take you 25 minutes, rather longer than Bond's frantic, 15-minute hurtle. As centre stage for a key scene in one of the most instantly recognised movie series in popular culture, this bustling Canterbury Road clearly captured Fleming's imagination.

Address Old Dover Road, CT1 3JB | Getting there 12-minute walk from Canterbury West station via St Peter's Street and the High Street, then turn right at Fenwick; Whitefriars car park | Hours Unrestricted | Tip Higham Park, on the edge of Bridge, was once home to the flamboyant motor-racing driver and car engineer Count Louis Zborowski, whose built cars fitted with aero engines were the inspiration behind Fleming's *Chitty Chitty Bang Bang*.

37 __ The Parade

Cornering Canterbury's wealth

Key corner sites of this stretch in central Canterbury were once in the hands of the city's influential monastic houses, which included St Augustine's (see ch. 43). Acquisitions of these sites on what is now commonly referred to as the Parade by shrewd clerics – most notably here by the powerful Benedictine Christ Church Priory – enabled them to influence the city's commercial developments.

Today, the Parade is a thriving retail crossroads, but during medieval times its central position marked it out as a significant point on the processional route from the royal castle to the cathedral. Pilgrims would find their way to Becket's tomb and the nearby inns, shops and main markets were filled with life. By the 20th century, jewellers, milliners and drapers were established here and in the surrounding area. Today's shops include quality fashion and shoe chains with bistros and cafés restoring flagging shoppers.

Until Whitefriars (see ch. 55) was established, one corner of the 20th-century Parade was occupied by the city's main Boots, credited with saving that building from possible demolition and for its sympathetic reconstruction in 1931. Not only that, until 1959/1960 the chemist even included a library in its store, which chimed with the legacy of booksellers in this area. The current occupiers, Pret A Manger, have respected the past as well. Next to the street name on the first floor you'll see the old Boots sign, under the weathered timber windows. Equally respectful is the fact that the Parade's TSB branch does not have a hole-in-the-wall cashpoint. This 20th-century convenience was not installed so as not to interfere with the historic building's aesthetic qualities.

A sweet shop is now situated on the nearby site of the former Chequer of Hope inn, whose original stone arcading and lion badge, said to be the mark of the fearless Black Prince, are evident on its exterior.

Address CT1 2JL | Getting there 12-minute walk from Canterbury West station via St Peter's Street and through the High Street; Whitefriars car park | Hours Exterior unrestricted | Tip Nearby Mercery Lane, exceedingly narrow, crackling with history, is home to the oldest houses in Canterbury. It is said to be the most photographed street in England and is where pilgrims would buy souvenirs of their visit.

38__ The Pig
Rock of ages

Celebrated diarist Samuel Pepys namechecks Bridge Place's founder, Sir Arnold Braems, as a dining companion and *bon vivant*. Sir Arnold's enthusiasm for the good life was legendary and the house he built on this site circa 1638 attracted high society. It also caught the eye of artists from all over Europe who created oil impressions of it. Its closest rival in grandeur and popularity with the aristocracy was Chilham (see ch. 11) but poor maintenance and high living took their toll, and the house was sold in 1704 to the neighbouring Brisons estate.

For reasons that remain unclear to this day (envy was cited) the new owners tore the main building down, sparing the wing you see now. After a few hundred more years of fun followed by neglect, the building was restored in the swinging 1960s by resourceful jazz enthusiast and promoter Peter Malkin, as a club venue called The Bridge Place Country Club. The Kinks, The Yardbirds and The Moody Blues all performed here; Led Zeppelin walked away with just £100 in 1968 for a sparsely attended gig. Canterbury and its environs were traditionally deprived of clubs and late-night licences at the time, possibly under the influence of the cathedral. This, and the semi-rural isolation of the place – three miles from Canterbury city centre – made the hedonism of this rock 'n' roll pile irresistible.

As musical trends changed, so did the club and in the 1970s and 1980s the sounds of soul and disco reverberated within. Relationships blossomed under the disco balls to the tunes played by big-name DJs. Malkin organised a final club night in 2017 and put the place on the market. In 2018 it underwent another revamp and has been reborn as part of the upmarket Pig chain. The new owners have kept the ample fireplaces and secret staircases and have even created a clutch of hop pickers' huts to evoke the Kentish agricultural heritage of oast houses (see ch. 21) and hop production.

MEET OUR ANIMALS

PIGS	WILD BOAR x KUNE KUNE	2
EWES	ROMNEY MARSH + 1 x TEXAL	18
LAMBS	ROMNEY MARSH	24

Address Bourne Park Road, Bridge, CT4 5BH, +44 (0)344 225 9494, www.thepighotel.com/at-bridge-place | **Getting there** 2-mile walk from Bekesbourne station or 10-minute drive from Canterbury; parking on-site | **Hours** Exterior unrestricted; enquire within or see website for accommodation and dining | **Tip** Nearby Bekesbourne was the birthplace of film director Michael Powell – part of the influential Powell and Pressburger cinematic team whose *A Canterbury Tale* was partially filmed in Fordwich (see ch. 20).

39 — Queningate and City Walls
Another brick in the wall

Canterbury was already a regional capital and administrative centre when the Romans established a settlement on the site around 70 AD. By the end of the 1st century, a town with a street grid had evolved, and by 275 AD a town of 120 acres was enclosed by a wall, backed by an earthen rampart and fronted by a wide ditch. Fragments of these Roman walls survive, with the chunky Queningate – a sturdy example of this form of early city planning – impossible to miss. Queen Bertha would make an entrance via the now blocked-up gate on her way to worship at St Martin's (see ch. 12). Tradition recounts that it owes its name to the future saint. It is partly visible, as is some of an original Roman brick in the masonry.

Not just a city landmark, the gate's key position made it an important site for Roman-era markets. Canterbury overall was an important trading centre in East Kent at the time but Queningate's 'flesh shambles' were later to thrive at the Buttermarket (see ch. 4) well into the medieval period. And it's hard to imagine now, but from 1851 the area was home to a brewery. It made way for a car park and toilets nearby when it was demolished in 1931. Intricate iron work points to its huge £2,300 cost, immense for the time. Now home to a 1920s Prohibition-style bar, you can descend its steps for daring cocktails.

Back in daylight, pass through Queningate's unblocked entrance for the Kent War Memorial Garden, which was a bowling green until 1921. Its obelisk is often missed by visitors, but no such thing could be said of Queningate itself; it has helped travellers map their routes to major nearby destinations for centuries. Having established the city's roughly ovoid form, after World War II Queningate and the city's walls (many of them rebuilt in the medieval period) helped shape Canterbury's modern ring road system and aided defence over the centuries.

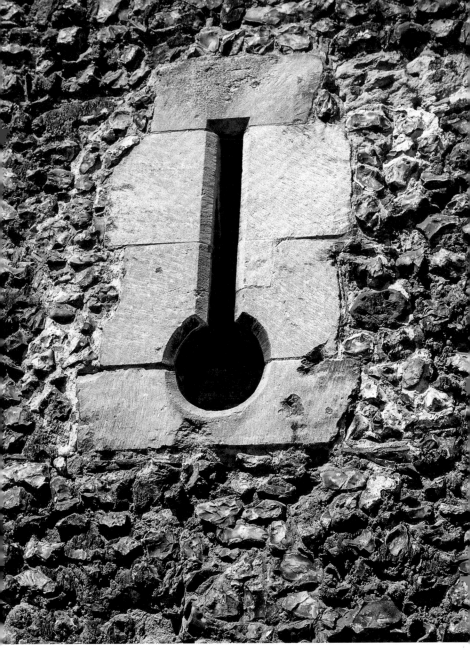

Address 21 Lower Bridge Street, CT1 2LX | Getting there 10-minute walk from Canterbury East station via Upper Bridge Street then left at the junction; Queningate car park | Hours Unrestricted | Tip Canterbury Castle's medieval keep is a prominent sight at the Wincheap junction. By the 12th century the castle's importance had waned as nearby Dover castle flourished and portions of it underwent demolition in the late 18th century.

40___Red Pump Well
Ancient sources, ancient courses

Look up in Canterbury and you'll see grinning gargoyles and timbered roofs. You will also come across this red pump on the side of the alternative shop Siesta Crafts. A fine reconstruction, it points to the role of this part of the city as the site of an ancient rush-market. Sweet-smelling rushes and other herbs and grasses were used as floor coverings in the medieval period, long before the use of carpets became commonplace. Rushes were environmentally friendly long before Extinction Rebellion and kept floorings fresh. It is fitting, then, that it is affixed to an ethically minded shop.

To keep these rushes fresh, water was drawn from a well in the street behind the pump. Because the water was tinged slightly red from the iron salts of the local springs, it was referred to as the Red Well or Red Pump. Pious city folk thought that the red colour came from the blood of murdered Becket. The Canterbury of the Middle Ages would have faced the same difficulties of meeting water supply as many parts of the world are experiencing now, and disputes regarding its provision were commonplace.

For another key part of Canterbury's water supply, head to St Augustine's Conduit House. In the second half of the 12th century, Prior Wilbert devised an elaborate system of pipes made out of lead or hollowed-out trees that ran from a spring at the conduit. The water made its way through settling tanks to be held in a water tower just north of the cathedral, supplying the priory with water for drinking, cooking, washing, and sewage removal. Previously, Roman public baths were commonplace.

As for the Red Pump Well, no one is sure when it fell into disuse, but it appears to have been rediscovered sometime in 1870. Its presence would have delighted locals in its assistance in providing clues as a pre-modern time facilitator for something many of us take for granted still.

Address 1 Palace Street, CT1 2DY | Getting there 10-minute walk from Canterbury West station; Queningate car park | Hours Unrestricted | Tip The tiny Zoar Strict & Particular Baptist Chapel lies in a bastion tower on the eastern side of Burgate Lane, and previously housed a city water cistern. The exterior of this unusual church is always unrestricted, but the interior is not open to the public.

41 The Roper Gateway
Sweet dreams are made of this

This huge, Grade II listed, 16th-century gate once introduced the way to the home of Margaret Roper, and a gruesome bit of Canterbury history.

Roper was the daughter of Sir Thomas More, Henry VIII's Lord Chancellor, who caused alarm in establishment circles with his influential socio-political satire, *Utopia*. If that wasn't enough to incur the wrath of the frequently vengeful king, More also refused to recognise both the king's role as Head of the Church of England and the annulment of his marriage to the first of his six wives. Like many unlucky enough to anger the tempestuous Tudor, More was beheaded in 1535 at Tower Hill, and in the practice of the time his head was displayed at London Bridge. Margaret bribed the executioner to save the head before it was thrown in the river. She is said to have then pickled it in spices and surrounded it with rose petals, storing it under her bed until she died in 1544. More's skull, Margaret and her husband were interred in the Roper family vault in the Church of St Dunstan (almost opposite the gateway). Not merely a devoted daughter, Margaret was a trailblazer. Highly educated and a keen linguist, she bucked the practice of the time for women to be versed in little else but family duties, and was the first non-royal woman to publish a book she had herself translated into English. As for her father, he was canonised in 1935 and is the patron saint of difficult marriages!

The gate is an example of decorative Tudor red-brickwork particular to Kent, deviating from the style in other southern counties. The bricks were laid in a method known as English bond and would have been fired and distributed throughout the structure. While the whole structure is now less imposing than the surrounding buildings, the wooden gate dwarfs the nearby doors, and the wonderful brickwork puts the modern buildings to shame.

Address St Dunstan's Street, CT2 8DA | Getting there 5-minute walk turning right from Canterbury West station; Canterbury West station car park | Hours Unrestricted | Tip St Dunstan Church holds what many say is the oldest working bell in Kent – maybe even the country. Thought to have been created in 1325, it is one of the few ancient bells that still regularly ring the changes in the English style instead of sitting silent in a museum.

42 Sainsbury's
A broad church for the city shopper

The huge Sainsbury's surrounded by other big retail names on the outskirts of the Canterbury is an indication that shopping may be the new religion in more ways than one.

Architects Ahrends, Burton and Koralek claimed that the highly unusual roof, suspended from soaring uprights, was created in 1984 to pay homage to the towers of the Canterbury cathedral, but locals were unconvinced and muttered about how much better the large store would look once the roof was in place. Others considered it a modern marvel.

Whatever your opinion, there is absolutely no missing it. Its sheer size makes it one of the most arresting buildings in the area. It was also the first high-profile store of the well-known chain to take on high-technology specifications. The traditional Sainsbury's style was updated, and although other outlets nearby are also high-tech in specification, it still looks fresh. The vast undivided interior feels like a hallowed space.

Despite its controversial beginnings, it has managed to win several awards. Interestingly, commenters have noted that such a building would be unlikely to achieve planning permission today. It is in fact surprising that it was built at all, as earlier on in their career Prince Charles described one of the architects' projects as a 'monstrous carbuncle'. This arose during a famous and controversial intervention during a planned wing of London's National Gallery. The publicity surrounding that project led to it being scrapped. Luckily, this fate was not bestowed on this store, and for a food shop you cannot go wrong here. Its offerings represent a microcosm of contemporary Canterbury, including spices and smoky sausages for the Chinese and Polish population living throughout the city. Even if the design is lost on you, this is a shop for everyone. Shopping may well be the new religion, and if it is, let us pray.

Address Kingsmead Road, CT1 1BW, +44 (0)1227 456860, www.stores.sainsburys.co.uk/ 0046/canterbury | Getting there 4-minute drive from the city centre; free car park on site | Hours Exterior unrestricted; Mon–Fri 7am–10pm, Sat 7am–9pm, Sun 10am–4pm | Tip The present Superdrug store in St George's Street was once the butcher and grocery store, David Grieg. The 1954 design was prepared in just five weeks and also divided opinion, with many speaking out against modern architecture in the city centre.

43 St Augustine's Abbey
Christianity's Kentish headquarters

When Pope Gregory chose Saint Augustine (then Augustine of Rome) to lead a mission to Christianise Britain, he sent him straight to Kent. The city was the seat of King Ethelbert of Kent and his wife, Frankish princess Bertha, who was already a devoted Christian. Augustine arrived in Canterbury circa 597, and it took a few years to convert the king, but then King Ethelbert granted him a piece of land on which he established a monastic community with the 40 monks who had accompanied him. The Benedictines flourished here and, as is well known, Augustine became the first Archbishop of Canterbury.

Monasteries and churches would have been a very desirable place for burial. However, the privilege was restricted to dignitaries and ecclesiastical figures, and only certain people managed to secure their final resting place within a site such as this. Among those interred here were the early archbishops and both Ethelbert and Bertha. (Several existing graves are still present, although making out their inscriptions is a little tricky.) With time, anyone showing the church sufficient largesse could be interred in one too. The bones of the dead would often be located close to where the monks prayed. Tombs were also strategically located on processional pathways and in front of altars or images of the saints to maximise the intercessory process – prayers to aid the living beneficiaries of a gift.

Despite being a maze of ancient relics, there is a peace here suited to its early role. Thirsty monks would have entered the spacious crypt for relaxation after a vegetarian dinner washed down with some ale. The peals of the campanile would have rung out over the neighbouring farm that supplied the monastic needs, and the surrounding area. The abbey since suffered theft, destruction and decay, but existing ruins provide ample evidence of the once flourishing community.

Address Longport, CT1 IPF | Getting there 12-minute walk from Canterbury East station via Rhodaus Town and Upper Bridge Street then right into Church Street and then Longport; Longport car park | Hours Daily 10am–5pm | Tip Once an important lynchpin of the royal and ecclesiastical ceremonial route, Lady Wootton's Green (see ch. 27) features two expressive statues of Bertha and Ethelbert unveiled by local sculptor Stephen Melton in 2006.

44__ St George's Place
This one will run rings round you

A modern stretch in a city vibrant with medieval and Georgian buildings, St George's Place provides an insight into how the city could have looked if some post-World War II planners had had their way. Before the bombing, it had distinguished itself as 'Doctor's Row' due to the vast number of doctors based there. But the reinvention of St George's Place started before the Luftwaffe hit.

In the early 20th century, Canterbury's urban planners swept away many slums and residential buildings, relocating their inhabitants to outer areas of the city. This, followed by the devastating bombings of 1942, meant a great deal of change.

In 1943, architect Dr Charles Holden was tasked with reconstructing the city. In 1945 he proposed a 'modernist utopia' with a large relief road cutting through the city as its lynchpin. Unsurprisingly, he faced fierce opposition from local groups and residents. Town and Country Minister Lewis Silkin grew tired of the squabbling and issued an ultimatum – come up with a solution or the council would decide. The warring factions joined forces and the more modern parts of Canterbury began to take shape, with St George's Place being a notable example.

To access St George's Place as a pedestrian via the city centre, you will have to navigate the ring road circuit constructed in the 1960s. Making this journey takes you into another Canterbury entirely – one featuring wide spaces between the buildings and a relative lack of tourists. Yet there are echoes of pre-modern Canterbury in the Baptist Church dating back to 1865 and clusters of Regency terraced houses. But the 20th century is the star here, with the 1970s Charter House and 1980s Waitrose supermarket. Joining the University of Kent and its Templeman Library (see ch. 51), this stretch broke with the vernacular of traditional Canterbury, and the city proved it could be contemporary too.

Address CT1 1UT | Getting there 15-minute walk from Canterbury West station via
the city centre and past Fenwick through the mural displays of the St George's underpass;
Longport car park | Hours Unrestricted | Tip Other examples of architecture diverging from
traditional styles and materials include Lloyds Bank (16th-century influences), Nat West
Bank (Italian palazzo façade) and the Beaney Institute (Art and Crafts).

45   St Thomas of Canterbury

A sanctuary with remembrance at its core

Come to this quiet, sparsely visited church for a chance to look at relics of its murdered patron saint in the peace of the Martyrs Chapel. Prepare to be disarmed by the sight of a scrap of his vestment robe and a piece of bone from his body, which was presented to the church over a hundred years ago. The experience offers a glimpse of his life and untimely death, free from the crowds that you might imagine flocking to see such poignant artefacts. It was the first Roman Catholic church in Canterbury since the Reformation. Until that time, local Catholics had worshipped over a mile away at the Hales Place chapel. So, it is a place with strong connections to those who have faced opposition for their faith.

Opened in 1875, the church is an example of Victorian Gothic, influenced by noted architect Augustus Pugin, with a 1962 modern extension on the left side. A large mural behind the altar in the extension depicts the sending to England of St Augustine, the first Archbishop of Canterbury. The high altar returns to the church's namesake with one relief displaying the martyrdom of St Thomas and one of his nemesis, King Henry II, performing public penance for uttering the words that led to Becket's brutal murder (see ch. 14). On either side of this area are two distinctive chapels: the Lady Chapel, featuring statues of St George and Saint Constance, and Saint Joseph's Chapel. This church also recognizes modern-day saints. Near Becket's artefacts in the Martyrs' Chapel are vestments (an alb and stole) belonging to Oscar Romero, Archbishop of San Salvador, who was assassinated in 1980 celebrating Mass. He was canonized in 2018 and, like Becket, he spoke out against poverty and social injustice and paid the ultimate price. Joining these touching displays are stained-glass windows commemorating soldiers killed in action in World War I. Reflect in peace on those who have suffered here.

Address 59 Burgate, CT1 2HJ, +44 (0)1227 462 896, www.stthomasofcanterbury.com,
canterbury@rcaos.org.uk | Getting there 12-minute walk from Canterbury West station via
St Dunstan's Street and the High Street then left at Mercery Lane and right onto Burgate;
Queningate car park | Hours Mass: Mon–Thu noon, Fri noon & 7.30pm, Sat noon & 6pm,
Sun 8, 9.30 & 11am, 4 (Polish) & 6pm | Tip Becket is not Canterbury's only saint. Saint
Alphege, canonized in 1078, was murdered by invading Danes after refusing to permit them
their ransom. The church that bears his name in Palace Street is not open to the public, but
the guesthouse on the same street is.

46__Sidney Cooper Gallery

Where Rupert Bear leaped off the page

This elegant 19th-century building is named after a celebrated local artist who specialized in depicting cattle. For a taste of his large canvases see the ground floor of The Beaney House of Art & Knowledge at 18 High Street. This building, though, was formally opened by Cooper in March 1868 as the Sidney Cooper Gallery of Art (later the Canterbury College of Art and School of Architecture). Today it's a large gallery space affiliated with Canterbury Christ Church University and has a rotating display of exhibitions, many of which celebrate local artists. It is reminiscent of a Grecian temple and looks polished and grand amongst the more regular shops and cafés nearby. To the right stands the house in which Cooper lived. He continued to act as a benefactor to the city, funding a theatre amongst other endeavours.

Generous Cooper funded and developed the gallery initially as a school to help those with artistic talent who might not be able to afford to study. Its most notable alumna was Mary Tourtel, who sketched a jaunty bear complete with checked trousers and yellow scarf following the encouragement of her husband, the then News Editor of the *Daily Express*. Rupert Bear was a brave and resourceful bear that cheered many spirits. In his heyday, Rupert was as ubiquitous as Harry Potter, and Tourtel's talents are remembered more fondly today than Cooper's immense agricultural canvases. Mary Tourtel died in 1948 and is buried in St Martin's churchyard (see ch. 12).

Cooper does get some respect, though. Outside the Sidney Cooper Gallery lies a Walter Cozens paving stone commemorating the artist. In the early 20th century Cozens, a local builder, initiated a scheme for laying paving stones to herald Canterbury's famed historical features. Dotted around the city's landmarks they can be spied at both Greyfriars (see ch. 23) and the Roper Gateway (see ch. 41), but are very easy to miss.

Address Sidney Cooper Gallery, 22–23 St Peter's Street, CT1 2BQ, +44 (0)1227 453267, www.canterbury.ac.uk/arts-and-culture/sidney-cooper-gallery | **Getting there** 8-minute walk from Canterbury West station, past Westgate Gardens towards the city centre; Whitefriars car park | **Hours** Exterior unrestricted; exhibitions Tue–Fri 10.30am–5pm, Sat 11.30am–5pm | **Tip** Craving your own bespoke bear? Make an appointment with Canterbury Bears in Littlebourne and they will create one bear for you using traditional Victorian methods of creativity, sustainable materials and German mohair (www.canterburybears.com).

47__Skinned Bull Sculpture
Sculpture to take you by the horns

Evidence of Canterbury's tanning and leather heritage is scant, but this sculpture of a fighting bull by Kent-based artist Steven Portchmouth features a stripped-back body, acknowledging how such animals have been exploited for their hides. Even naked like this, though, the bull exudes the legendary strength of an intact animal. Portchmouth left the bull's face unskinned in order that he might give him an expression of pride.

The sculpture stands in Tannery Field, in the depths of Westgate Parks. Here once lay the 'slub' bank for the overflowing waste of much of Canterbury's leather industry. Tanneries tended to favour the quality of bull hides over cow hides. Locals still remember the noxious smell of the slub drifting over the city at regular intervals, stopping people in their tracks.

The actual train gauge of the tannery railway that forms much of Portchmouth's sculpture was discovered by Westgate Parks volunteers when they were installing the wildflower meadow here. It offers a rare glimpse of the industry's infrastructure. The Williamson family established the tannery in the 1790s and stood at the helm for two centuries. The city's leather industry flourished during the Napoleonic threat of the late 18th century, when three large barracks housed over 3,000 troops, all needing boots and harnesses. The company also supplied leather for the House of Lords, Rolls-Royce, Jaguar and also – allegedly – for the chair from the television quiz show *Mastermind*.

Portchmouth originally planned to make this bull angry, because 'we've skinned his whole species, ever since the beginning'. Instead, he imagined a happy life for him, with no consciousness that he was skinned for profit. And now, with railway tracks as his exposed muscles and a challenge in his eyes, he serves as a reminder of what both the field and innumerable animals like himself have been used for.

Address Tannery Field, Westgate Parks, CT1 2BQ | Getting there 10-minute walk from Canterbury West station, access via the public footpath entrance off Rheims Way or from Bingley Estate or Old Tannery Development; Northgate car park | Hours Unrestricted | Tip At nearby Whitehall Meadows, a rare wet meadow and rugged space accessed via Whitehall Road, traditional conservation methods have created a magnet for migratory birds such as snipe and teal.

48 Solly's Orchard
The apple of Canterbury's eye

Henry III was a generous benefactor to a band of Dominican brothers and sisters. Saint Dominic of Spain passed through the south of France on a diplomatic mission and was shocked to encounter heretical activities. After establishing his order in Toulouse, he and his spiritual wanderers did not confine themselves to their cloisters like contemplative monks, but spread their message of religion and obedience within communities. They were particularly drawn to cities where they could make maximum impact. The Dominicans – also known as Black Friars – who headed for this site made their way to Canterbury from Dover on foot. With their bounty they eagerly built a priory within Canterbury's city walls starting in 1236. Other monarchs were not so benevolent. Henry VIII, whose reign began in 1509, had most of the buildings on this site destroyed by 1538, but it is still possible to get an external view of the flint refectory, which has gone through various incarnations. In the 1700s it was an Anabaptist (later Unitarian) meeting house; in 1912, a storehouse.

Fast-forward to the 21st century. In 2007, 14 three-year-old apple trees were planted to re-establish the former orchard here. These trees were christened Chorister Boy and the Ten Commandments amongst others to evoke the area's Catholic connections. And with local cidery Rough Old Wife on board, these juicy apples have been pressed into drinks which follow the policy of ensuring fruit is collected from unsprayed trees. Even better, a profit percentage is ploughed into local environmental funds.

Nowadays, the site is a green and peaceful place flecked with sweet woodruff, perennial violas and ferns. The gentle lap of the Stour can be heard. Although the Black Friars do not have a brick-and-mortar presence in the city anymore, as itinerant preachers they have left their indelible mark on the city.

Address Entrance opposite The Millers Arms, 2 Mill Lane, CT1 2AW | Getting there 10-minute walk from Canterbury West station past Westgate Towers and St Peter's Street then left down St Peter's Lane; St Radigund's car park | Hours Unrestricted | Tip The tiny walled butterfly garden nearby was created in 1983 after the demolition of two 19th-century cottages. Look out for crocuses, snowdrops and winter aconites followed by tulips and daffodils when it gets warmer.

49_ Stour Street

Brewing up a storm

If you're on your way to the High Street or Greyfriars (see ch. 23), why not take in Stour Street on your way? Often narrow, sometimes curving, sometimes cobbled, it offers many clues to the city's historical products. Tanned hides, for example. At the southwest end of the street, glance down tiny Church Lane toward the 11th-century St Mildred's Church, next to which stood a busy Victorian tannery. Nearby place names such as Drying Shed Lane point to this industrial heritage. About halfway along the street, the impressive flint and stone, 12th-century Poor Priests Hospital housed a tannery before being rebuilt as the residence of wealthy minter and moneylender Lambin Frese. Stour Street was formerly called Lamb Lane, possibly a reference to his importance. A hospital for poor priests from the mid-13th century, the building later became a prison and a poor-house, and in the Victorian era was a workhouse. It is now home to the Marlowe Kit, hosting a wide range of creative and heritage activities celebrating Kent's stories and storytellers.

Stour Street was also once alive with ale and stout fermentation, and pubs. Number 42, a partially black-and-white structure built in the 1640s, was once a merchant's home but was also the Royal Exchange Inn. Now called Royal Exchange House, it is a holiday home for rent. Just before the hospital you will pass Beer Cart Lane, which would have been lined with brewers' drays and pubs. The Old Brewery Business Centre at number 75 formed part of a local brewery empire until the mid-Victorian era and is now offices. At what is now the Foundry Brew Pub at number 77, cast metal was smelted. Step inside for their Torpedo ale named in honour of the foundry's torpedo production. When you approach the end of Stour Street, you'll be next to the Abode hotel, whose ancient beams are on view inside the reception. In the 1840s, the very back of the hotel was a pub named the Prince Albert in honour of Queen Victoria's husband.

Address CT1 2PJ | **Getting there** 2-minute walk from Canterbury Castle, 14-minute walk from Canterbury West station; Castle Street car park | **Hours** Unrestricted | **Tip** In the 12th century, the wealthy Mayner the Rich founded almshouses on Hospital Lane for the elderly poor. Now called Maynard and Cotton's Hospital, it continues to accommodate residents in need. The Dutch-style gabled roof can be viewed from Stour Street.

50__ Sun Street

Overlapping tiles, overlapping histories

Sun Street once included an auctioneer, perfumers, a haberdasher and a straw bonnet warehouse. Look upwards towards the medieval storeyed buildings – during the Middle Ages these would have been rented out to tenants. Lower your gaze and you can still view the decorative mosaics that led the way to some of these historic traders. A colourful one greets you at the entrance of the former long-established family menswear business Deakins. Its heritage is now reflected in the name of the friendly Draper's Arms pub which occupies the original site. The high-quality shops and bistros here and at the Guildhall Street island reflect the well-heeled nature of this part of Canterbury today as well. Bespoke jewellers join handmade sweet shops and independent cafés, and the cobbled streets slow the pace.

Here and there you'll also see the mathematical tiles which were a popular architectural feature of 18th-century Kent and Sussex. Overlapping tiles in hues of terracotta, black and white, they are found on many of the properties in Canterbury's shopping streets. Attached to wooden battens, they fool the eye into thinking they are bricks. They were cost effective, weather hardy and did not require the skill of the bricklayer.

One building which has almost escaped modernisation entirely is the timbered frame of the Sun Hotel, which dates back to 1503, while the surrounding buildings are in the 19th-century mock-Tudor style. Step inside to view the low ceilings and beams. The Sun Hotel also managed to survive a huge fire in 1865. Its previous incarnation as the Little Inn was referenced by Charles Dickens, but whether it was this hotel that he mentions in *David Copperfield* or another hotel nearby that shared the same name remains under debate. The writer was fond of this city, and once read his work at the now demolished Theatre Royal.

Address CT1 2HX | **Getting there** 10-minute walk from Canterbury West station via the High Street before turning right at Mercery Lane; Queningate car park | **Hours** Exterior unrestricted | **Tip** Kent became a centre for brick and tile manufacture in Roman times. In medieval times, tiles and pottery were made at Tyler Hill and other nearby surrounding areas. You may still be able to spot fragments of tiles in the ground as well as traces of clay pits.

51 Templeman Library
Gleaming addition to the city

Myriad ancient structures are dotted around Canterbury with the cathedral being the most obvious. But here, high on the city's peak, stands a gleaming chunk of modernity forming a pivotal part of the University of Kent. Originally created by architect William Holford in the 1960s, this library (and the other buildings which surround it) brought the then-startling, in-your-face ethos of Brutalism to this genteel city. It is the newly refreshed library which stands out as the most arresting – and sparkling. It is almost as if a piece of London's Canary Wharf had been towed down into the Garden of England.

Funny to think that E. L. James of *Fifty Shades of Grey* fame would have picked up her history texts here during her time at the university. She is just one of the learning centre's many impressive alumni. Oh my.

Although the University of Kent is firmly of the now, this library manages to reference the cathedral with repeating brick bays buttressing the building. In stark green and brown, it stands out amongst the more sober grey Lego-like blocks here. Neat sheets of grass surround the building and the paving surrounding it gives it a sense of castle-like solitude. The library is thoroughly modern, but the interior is not completely tech-ed out. There are over a million lovely books and yes, computers too, but print fans can gain traction in the knowledge that the archives are temperature and moisture controlled. There is also a bundle of cartoon memorabilia celebrating the best of British examples of the art which has reflected societal trends. Some 200,000 original artworks are held here dating back centuries and it is free to access, but a few days' notice is usually required.

Travel back into the city on a bio-fuelled bus making its way down the peak for some picture-postcard scenes of the city and its more celebrated sights, but don't forget the cathedral of learning right here.

Address University of Kent, Library Road, CT2 7NU, +44 (0)1227 824777, www.kent.ac.uk/is/templeman | **Getting there** Unibus or bus 4 to the University; permit required for parking on site | **Hours** Daily 8am–9pm | **Tip** Catch a show at the Gulbenkian theatre, also part of the university, and offering both serious and silly entertainment since 1969 (www.thegulbenkian.co.uk).

52__ Water Tower
A dark past but a bright future

A striking Victorian residence with sympathetic interior design features. Sounds idyllic? Perhaps not so much for the previous inhabitants who would have sheltered in its adjacent buildings. For this spectacular water tower was a feature of one of Kent's most controversial psychiatric hospitals. Founded in 1872 with space for 1,205 patients, the immense asylum (to use the language of the time) on the sprawling Chartham Downs lent itself well to self-sufficiency. It incorporated a farm making ample use of a local orchard and hops. Joining this was a baker, butcher, cricket team and even a cemetery and a chapel of rest.

During World War II, the hospital laundry provided the steam for the Chartham air-raid siren, and one wing of the hospital was adapted for use intended as a makeshift military hospital. In 1948 it became part of the NHS, renamed St Augustine's Hospital. It is under this name that it became notorious. In the 1970s, a University of Kent researcher drew attention to the treatment of patients in its care. The casual administering of practices such as electroconvulsive therapy (attaching wires to the head designed to treat depression) and other invasive treatments were highlighted, among other types of abuse and neglect.

St Augustine's was closed in 1993 as another controversy emerged – that of the community care programme, which still attracts dissenters. Many of its buildings were either torn down or scheduled for housing. The chapel and this elegant water tower were retained and incorporated into the sought-after and expensive St Augustine's Estate. Chartham Hatch village is just over a mile away and includes the UK's first orchard to be defined a Local Wildlife Orchard. No Man's Community Orchard, so named because it falls between two parishes, is filled with traditional varieties of Kentish apples, springtime blossoms and lichens.

Address Beech Avenue, Chartham, CT4 5RU | Getting there 5-minute train journey from Canterbury West station and then 4-minute walk to Chilham, then bus 1a or train for 32 minutes and a 23-minute walk; Chartham Village Hall car park | Hours Exterior unrestricted | Tip St Thomas' Hill Water Tower on Whitstable Road in Canterbury is a stark white edifice built in 1927. Decommissioned in 1998, it now attracts photographers drawn to its distinctive outline.

53__Weir Bridge
This wheel's on fire

Take a detour away from Canterbury's crowds to where local industries kept the city supplied with flour, paper and cotton. Although Abbotts Mill, second in size only to the cathedral, was lost to a savage fire in 1933, there's enough history within this watery 'island' to take you back to the time when Canterbury's powerhouse served the city.

Until the dissolution of the monasteries, earlier mills on the site were owned by the monks of St Augustine's Abbey (see ch. 43) who produced grain and hemp. Abbotts Mill, designed by civil engineer John Smeaton, was completed in 1792 and cost £8,000. Alderman James Simmons, a prominent local businessman and instrumental figure in transforming Dane John Gardens (see ch. 16), engaged Smeaton for the project. Although Smeaton, who also designed the iconic Eddystone lighthouse, died before his vision was realised, his talents were put to optimum use. The machinery adopted was highly advanced for the time, with metal rather than timber forming the mill's components.

At six storeys high and with an octagonal turret, this mill was a local landmark. Look carefully for some of Smeaton's legacy, such as the spindle on one of the wheels and two iron pillars. The mill pond, 1829 date marker on the weir bridge and water height stone offer insight into the mill's golden days before the devastating fire.

The Miller's Arms pub on Mill Lane features several paintings of Abbot's Mill before and during the huge blaze, which started during repainting and overwhelmed Smeaton's advanced construction techniques. Half a million gallons of water were needed to douse the flames. But the area is set to rise again with a renewable electricity source planned by harnessing the Stour. Other intended attractions for the Abbot's Mill Project include a vegan community café, permaculture woodland garden and wildlife shelters.

Address St Radigund's Street, CT1 2AA | **Getting there** 12-minute walk from Canterbury West station through to St Peter's Street, turning right onto Best Lane and towards Mill Lane; Pound Lane car park | **Hours** Unrestricted | **Tip** Nearby Pound Lane was where wool, brought by river for the use of Canterbury's weavers, was stored. Café du Soleil, also on Pound Lane, is a restaurant based in a former 18th-century wool store (www.cafedusoleil.co.uk).

54__Westgate Hall and Curzon
From combat to culture

Canterbury's village hall didn't start life as a place of cultural happenings. In fact, it had more to do with war than art, serving a drill hall from which the troops of the Territorial Army set off to the battlefields of World War I. The building later survived the 1944 bombings before evolving into a place of music and dance due to its beautiful wooden floor. Today it welcomes contemporary talent, but it is also notable as one of the few places left in the city where you will be able to summon up the psychedelic ghosts of the Canterbury scene.

The Canterbury scene, or 'Canterbury Sound', whose jazz and folk-rock blend of prog rock continues to inspire musicians today, flowered here. Spawned by the group The Wilde Flowers, who never released an album but led to the creation of other influential bands, the scene blossomed in the 1960s and 1970s with the playful participation of Herne Bay native Kevin Ayers (see ch. 71) and Canterbury stalwart Robert Wyatt, reaching its peak with bands like Caravan and Soft Machine. Robert Wyatt's childhood home in Lydden (outside Canterbury) is still in existence, and the musician was made an honorary Doctor of Music at the University of Kent in 2014.

Something of this countercultural vibe still flows here in the Curzon cinema, which shows left-of-centre and international films alongside the more standard blockbusters. Although the site has been updated, you can still find details from when it was originally built in 1913. The Curzon cinema foyer could be straight out of the movies itself, with its glamorous long bar and Art Deco fittings, plus cocktails such as watermelon-and-cucumber gin and tonic and peach tree sour. If you're a lady, visit the ladies' toilet and see the original window frames, delicately pretty despite the passage of time. Or simply admire the outside and the graceful windows that seem to spin the light.

Address Westgate Hall Road, CT1 2BT, +44 (0)333 321 0104, www.westgatehall.org, www.curzoncinemas.com/canterbury/info | Getting there 10-minute walk from Canterbury West station via Station Road, the High Street and St Peter's Lane; Pound Lane car park | Hours Check websites for event and movie times | Tip Just a 4-minute walk away, the Lady Luck pub has been hosting live music with an emphasis on acts outside the mainstream since the 1950s (www.theladyluck.co.uk).

55 __ Whitefriars

Dig for treasure – and lots more too

Between 2000 and 2003 the 'Big Dig' archaeological excavation was carried out here, at what is now the biggest shopping centre in East Kent. The Canterbury Archaeological Trust in conjunction with Channel 4's popular television programme *Time Team* unearthed finds dating back to the Iron Age and through the Roman, Anglo-Saxon and medieval eras. From mosaic floors and a friary cess pit to a hairpin of jet and a perfume bottle of glass, the thousands of finds have helped scholars understand how life was lived in early Canterbury.

Don't just imagine what's underground. Look up. Take in the high arches dominating Whitefriars Arcade (formerly Marlowe Arcade). Referencing the city's poet (see ch. 32) but with its walkway set firmly in the consumerist boom of 1980s Britain, Marlowe Arcade was completed in 1985. In 2004 Whitefriars was established, and the two sites are key areas of the city, with Fenwick department store now commanding the scene. Marlowe Arcade was renamed White-friars' Arcade in 2012. The elaborate neo-Georgian weathervane of the original Marlowe Theatre (see ch. 32) welcomes shoppers rather than theatre fans with its masks of tragedy and comedy, above the St Margaret's Street entrance. Look out for the uneven shaped red bricks (known as 'specials') and a plaque drawing attention to the original name. There is also an original sign at the link bridge between the car park and Primark.

If you think that these popular sites buzz with life, you'd be right, and not just about humans. Three hives were installed atop White-friars to help pollinate the city centre's flowers providing a home for 50,000 bees during summer. In 2012, the first batch of White-friars honey was produced, available on occasional days at Whitefriars Square, which links the two shopping areas and where you can also find other seasonal and local foods plus a thriving Christmas market.

Address 14 Gravel Walk, CT1 2TF | **Getting there** 12-minute walk from Canterbury West station via St Peter's Street and the High Street before turning into Rose Lane; for Whitefriars' Arcade turn right into Rose Square or enter via St Margaret's Street; Whitefriars car park | **Hours** Whitefriars Mon–Sat 9.30am–5.30pm, Sun 10am–4pm; Whitefriars' Arcade gates open daily 7am–9pm | **Tip** Adult shop Ann Summers is found on Gravel Walk between the two sites. A familiar addition to many shopping streets all over the country, this branch caused controversy in 2004 when it opened in a historically conservative city.

56 Wickhambreaux

Perfect for sheep … and royalty

It's hard to believe that this quiet village is just four miles away from busy Canterbury.

Wickhambreaux owes its unusual name to William de Breuse or Braose, who had familial roots in Normandy. The suffix 'breaux' was added to the Wickham name when he owned the manor in 1285. The landmark title that was the Domesday Book name-checked this village astride the Little Stour (see ch. 26) as part of its audit of England's wealth and taxes. Three hundred sheep called it their home when the book was published in its distinctive Medieval Latin in 1086.

The rural pull of the village attracted some notable names. Previous inhabitants include England's first Norman king, William the Conqueror, who gave the Kentish ragstone manor to his ruthless and ambitious half-brother Odo from Bayeaux in the 11th century. A large chunk of Wickhambreaux later passed into the hands of a woman, in the 14th century. The name of Joan, Countess of Kent is not widely recognised today, but her husband was the Black Prince who led several bloody military campaigns in France and Spain. At a time of politically motivated unions, the Black Prince's interest in her was based on love. She valued peace, won the respect of dissenters and came to be referred to as the 'Fair Maid of Kent'.

Quiet Wickhambreaux seems an unlikely former centre for the rowdy practice of 'hoodening'. One of the earliest recorded mentions of it was recorded by the Rev Pegge in his *Alphabet of Kenticisms* in 1735, although its origins may date back to the 5th century. Hoodeners were labourers who would knock on doors brandishing a wooden model hobby horse clamouring for Christmas money. Hoodening still breaks out for special events today, but the village is usually tranquil, and has attracted notable residents in more recent times too, such as Fleetwood Mac's Christine McVie.

Address CT3 1RQ | Getting there Bus 11 from Canterbury bus station; on-street parking | Hours Unrestricted | Tip The pretty church at nearby Littlebourne includes kaleidoscopic stained-glass windows designed by prominent Gothic Revivalist Nathaniel Westlake.

57__Wincheap
A win by any other name

With its name deriving either from the Saxon *Wenchiape*, a wine market, or the Old English *Waegnceap*, a wagon market, Wincheap long supported a lively rural economy. It hosted a timber market as early as the 13th century, and a cherry market that lasted until the early 19th century. It's no surprise that inns abounded, and Wincheap Road was home to a string of them, one of which, the 15th-century King's Head, is still very much a going concern. It is the oldest pub in Canterbury and the busy road it stands on is thought to have originated as part of an ancient trackway later to be exploited by the Romans as a route for ironworks via the forested Weald. Next to The King's Head you'll find the brick boundary wall of the Nonconformist burial ground. Created as a final resting place for Protestants dissenting from Anglicanism, it was open for burials between 1849 and 1938. Today it is a nature reserve.

Martyrs' Field Road, a 10-minute walk from The King's Head, is distinguished by a monument commemorating the death of the Canterbury Martyrs during the fractious medieval period when England was divided on religious grounds. During the short, violent, 16th-century reign of Mary I, who was also known as 'Bloody Mary', the Catholic daughter of Henry VIII was determined to rid the country of Protestants and did so in the most extreme way possible. The obelisk topped by the Canterbury Cross (see ch. 7) commemorates the final 41 of the thousands of English Protestants whom she had burned at the stake.

Modern Wincheap – including its surrounding suburban and urban sprawl – seems an unlikely corner of ancient roots. Unlike Canterbury's centre, where to look skywards is to be rewarded with gargoyles, green men and ancient signage, here you can look down for sections of York stone and at eye-level for early 19th-century cast-iron bollards and railings.

Address CT1 3TQ | Getting there 15-minute walk from Canterbury East station past the station bridge and in the direction of Wincheap or take bus 22 from the main depot; Maynard Road car park | Hours Unrestricted | Tip Few red telephone boxes are now in existence in Canterbury, but a Grade II listed cast-iron one of these quintessentially British designs can be found by Wincheap railway bridge.

In Memory of
FORTY-ONE KENTISH MARTYRS
WHO WERE
BURNT AT THE STAKE ON THIS SPOT
IN THE REIGN OF QUEEN MARY
A.D. 1555–1558

FOR THEMSELVES THEY EARNED THE MARTYR'S CROWN
BY THEIR HEROIC FIDELITY, THEY HELPED TO SECURE
FOR SUCCEEDING GENERATIONS THE PRICELESS BLESSING
OF RELIGIOUS FREEDOM.

"PRECIOUS IN THE SIGHT OF THE LORD IS THE DEATH OF HIS SAINTS"

58__ Ye Olde Beverlie

One trap you'll want to be caught in

Canterbury pubs are more than drinking dens. Over the centuries they have provided shelter for pilgrims, hosted Oddfellow meetings (see ch. 35) and their outdoor spaces were where an eccentric sport is still played today. Heats here date back to 1738, and many find it as fun to watch as to play. Called bat and trap, the game centres on two teams of six to ten players including substitutes. Key to bat and trap is a hard rubber ball (similar to those used in lacrosse) which the batsman aims from a rectangular box on the ground.

It is difficult to pinpoint the game's exact beginnings and some sources cite 13th-century origins. Regards the modern game, an updated version was popular as recuperation therapy after World War I for the many limbless servicemen returning home from the trenches. The game offered competitiveness and outdoor recreation without the more rigorous demands of cricket.

The Canterbury League was established in 1922 and was largely formed of teams who were based within walking distance of the city. As public transport improved, village teams took part contributing to the League's popularity. The League flourished, with prominent local business owners donating cups. In the 1930s it continued to win fans, until World War II brought about a hiatus. In 1946 the League were batting again, and by 1951 a major regulation was introduced – every league team had to have its pitch floodlit.

The League were the first sporting organisation in Britain to insist on this for its member clubs, implementing the rule four years before the same regulation was sanctioned by the Football Association. There are differently named variations of bat and trap all over the country, but it is much loved in Kent. And many other local pubs hold heats including the Smugglers Inn (see ch. 74). Why not attend one and see how much you think cricket and baseball owe to this ancient game?

Address St Stephen's Green, CT2 7JU, +44 (0)2227 463974, www.yeoldebeverlie.com |
Getting there Bus 21a from Canterbury bus station toward St Stephen's; parking on site |
Hours Daily noon–10pm | Tip The Spitfire Ground, St Laurence on the Old Dover
Road is home to one of the oldest cricket grounds in the country. Even today they play by
their own rules, which were adapted to take into account the ancient lime tree that once
dominated the pitch.

59   A Casa Mia

A slice of pizza, a slice of home

If you think that the pizzas here do taste and smell authentically Italian, then you'd be *corretto*.

This restaurant is the first in the UK to be certified by the Associazione Verace Pizza Napoletana, which is to say, these wise guys really know their dough.

Owner and chef Gennaro started out in the business young – as an unpaid delivery boy in Naples. On Sundays, his family would send him out to Lombardi to bring pizza home from their favourite pizzeria. He is now creating the sort of Italian food that really does live up to the restaurant's name – at my house – with a friendly welcome and relaxed style of service. Slow food if you like, and fit not just for a *casa* but also a *palazzo*.

Creating a Neapolitan pizza that meets all the necessary regulations is not easy, but A Casa Mia have aced it with hand-kneaded pizzas brimming with Kentish garden toppings. The magic happens in a huge, traditional domed Neapolitan pizza oven taking centre stage. 'A gas oven is less messy than a pizza oven,' shrugs Gennaro, but 'tradition is tradition.' He slides one of his creations out of the furnace; they are always made with soft-grain flour, sea salt and the juiciest, fruitiest olive oils. You can almost see Sophia Loren smile in approval from her vantage point on the wall.

Toppings focus on the traditional, such as salamis and artichokes. Fresh mussels from the local waters (as abundant as Kent's fields) turn up in starters and pasta dishes. Flavours are enhanced further by the addition of a grappa or craft cider or beer, or two.

Traditional Italian food is a rare find in this corner of the world, but at A Casa Mia you will experience an ode to Napoli to rival any metropolitan gastro scene. It is winning over locals as well as outsiders. With fresh, rustic décor and the scent of garlic in the air, it's a summery spot even on the greyest of days.

Address 160 High Street, CT6 5AJ, +44 (0)1227 372947, www.acasamia.co.uk | Getting there 12-minute walk from Herne Bay station through Memorial Park and onto the High Street; William Street car park | Hours Mon–Thu 5–11pm, Fri & Sat noon–3.30pm & 5–11.30pm, Sun noon–10pm | Tip You'll need plenty of pizza if you plan to complete the entire Via Francigena pilgrimage which includes religious sites in Canterbury as well as sections of France, Switzerland and Rome.

60 Amy Johnson Statue

An astonishing aviatrix, a mysterious end

This jaunty bronze statue created by Stephen Melton encapsulates the pioneering aviator at her peak. Complete with aviation gear and goggles she looks at ease, as she would have done when flying – the activity came so naturally to her.

The daughter of a Yorkshire fish exporter, Johnson made aviation history as the first woman to fly solo from England to Australia in 1930. Herne Bay's place in her story is not widely known, but the town was her last call before her fatal flight in 1941. Johnson's legacy as a heroine was cemented at the height of World War II when she bravely took off in dense fog in an Airspeed Oxford heading towards RAF Kidlington, near Oxford. When she veered off course and crashed into the Thames Estuary, severe weather conditions foiled all rescue attempts. Her body and aircraft have lain in freezing waters for more than eight long decades.

Diving enthusiasts based in Kent have taken up the challenge to discover the wreckage. Armed with witness reports, tide and weather charts for diving and photographs of the aircraft's structure the team are as prepared as they can possibly be. But it is not an easy task. The sediment in the waters means there is little or no light when trying to locate traces of the crash. Johnson was thought to have landed between two busy shipping lanes, and the traffic there will have disturbed the few clues thought to survive. Not only that, but the currents are unpredictable. Despite the discovery of the wreckage of a plane in 2003 in local waters, it was not thought to be the final resting place of Johnson, who keeps the secret of her tragic flight in her very watery grave.

Johnson's vigour and strong will is caught in the statue's gaze straight into the clouds. Female aviators remain rare today, as do statues of women. This lovely representation of a nation's heroine standing proud is a wonderful example of both.

Address Herne Bay promenade | Getting there 3-minute walk from Mortimer Street and then straight ahead to the promenade; Neptune car park | Hours Unrestricted | Tip Nearby is a picnic bench in the design of a biplane also commemorating the aviator. A fun place for lunch, Jane Priston's eye-catching bench was designed as part of a local art project.

61 Barnes Wallis Statue
An eccentric – and deadly – engineer

Perched precariously on the grassy slopes of the Downs stands a rather small statue devoted to the wartime engineer and inventor of the bouncing bomb (see ch. 63). Sometimes controversial, Barnes Wallis was a man who devised something that destroyed lives, so railings surround his likeness, protecting him from the threat of vandalism. Cast by sculptor Tom White, his likeness is assured as he gazes towards the coast where his most famous invention took off. Although he was not from the area, he lived in the town and realised that the isolation of Reculver was a prime spot to test his menacing, water-skipping invention. Although the statue looks as if it could tumble at any moment, Wallis's legacy is nowhere near as fragile.

He was convinced that to win World War II it was not necessary to demolish cities but to target power sources instead, and he aimed to obliterate German's vital dams. His theory proved to be a success and provided the template for the much-loved movie *The Dam Busters* with its rousing theme tune. The end of World War II didn't bring his inventions to an end. Even when he retired aged 83, he came up with wackier ideas such as swing-wing planes and hypersonic aircraft, making him a true pioneer. In a departure from the thinking that had made him famous, he also invented the non-misting glassless mirror – one of which was sold to Buckingham Palace. Like all good inventors, he was prone to eccentricity, for example eating only an exact amount of porridge and eight pruncs for breakfast.

In 1951, Wallis was given a grant of £10,000 by the Royal Commission on Awards to Inventors for his wartime work. He donated it to a hospital in Horsham to establish a trust to educate the children of RAF members killed or injured in action. Although he had damaged the lives of some with his famous invention, he came to enrich others with his legacy.

Address 2 Beacon Hill, CT6 6AU | Getting there Walk along the promenade towards Reculver until you reach the grassy Downs. He stands at the top; Reculver Country Park car park | Hours Unrestricted | Tip HSBC Bank in Herne Bay High Street is the site of the former War Shrine where, during World War I, local people went to remember their loved ones who had died or were still serving in the conflict.

62 Beach Creative

Life's a gas

This landmark building, now home to the Beach Creative arts centre, has always been in the business of energising Herne Bay. Built in 1899 as the offices of the local gas company and the house of its manager and his family, the site once also boasted two gas holders. In 1901, in what you might call an early exercise in street art, the company transformed the town with light, as a local news report recorded: 'This week the promenade at Herne Bay has burst forth in unwonted splendour after the sun has set, thanks to an installation of intensified incandescent gas lighting, which has just been completed by the Gas Company, to the order of the local authority.'

This illumination was too late for artist and poet Dante Gabriel Rossetti to observe. He visited the town for his health in 1877 and is memorialised in Beach Creative's Rossetti Room, which hosts classes for budding artists. But the gas lights must have helped to illuminate the 1913 stay of Dada artist Marcel Duchamp, whose urinal still raises a laugh and who also has his name on a gallery. An avid note-keeper, Duchamp attached a photograph of the illuminated pier (see ch. 77) to one of his notes, describing a possible background to his work in progress as 'An electric fête recalling the decorative lighting of Magic City or Luna Park, or the Pier Pavilion at Herne Bay.'

As with many sites here, the building undertook a new role during World War II when army and navy recruits were billeted here. These temporary residents included commandos who took part in the Normandy landings. Now the building soldiers on with multimedia exhibitions. Beach Creative retains reminders of the building's utilitarian past, and the café's serving hatch, where the gas workers once received their wages, now issues sardines on toast and other delights. Although the gas company is gone, this building still shines brightly.

Address Beach House, Beach Street, CT6 5PT, +44 (0)300 111 1913, www.beachcreative.org, www.beachcreativeinfo@gmail.com | Getting there 5-minute walk from Herne Bay station through the Memorial Park; Beach Street car park | Hours Exterior unrestricted; galleries and cafés: daily 10am–4pm | Tip If you are picking up a picnic at the nearby Morrisons, you can use their unusual customer-only rooftop car park, nip across the road to catch a bit of art, and then continue on to lunch.

63 Bouncing Bomb
A bombshell like no other

Strange to think that this small seaside town should be so pivotal in World War II history, but Reculver's remoteness made it the perfect place for testing the bouncing bomb. Prototypes were launched off the beach, and one of the gloriously eccentric Seaside Museum's exhibits includes a battered and rusty test explosive. The cylindrical bombs were invented in 1942 by Barnes Wallis, who came up with the idea of bouncing a round bomb across the water using marbles in a water tub in the back garden or in his bath, depending on which legend you prefer. His experiment contributed to resultant Allied victory and a much-loved movie *The Dam Busters*.

When testing began, secrecy and security shrouded the operation and police cordoned off the quiet stretch of coast at Reculver. High-speed cameras recorded the events. There is also footage of the operation in the museum. Initial testing proved to be unsuccessful, with 'Bomber' Harris maligning the plan as 'Tripe of the wildest description! Not the smallest chance of it working!' However, senior RAF officials were impressed, and the bombs were put to work destabilising Germany's dams. The resulting success was not without Allied heartbreak. Young, locally based pilot Warner 'Bill' Ottley flew on the famous raid and was killed.

And as for the real deal? An Upkeep bomb was found washed up on the shore on Reculver in 2018 much to the excitement of locals, some of whom called to keep it there as a kind of permanent artefact reminder of the war. Instead, it was taken here to the safe hands of this museum after being tested by explosives professionals. A coppery, rusty hunk now but it had the potential to cause huge devastation during the dark days of World War II.

But if you are a historical detective, why not look on the beach itself where bits of the bouncers wash up from time to time? Stand well back though!

Address Seaside Museum, 12 William Street, CT6 5EJ, +44 (0)1227 367368, www.theseasidemuseumhernebay.org | Getting there 3-minute walk from Mortimer Street, turning left onto William Street; William Street car park | Hours Tue–Sun 11am–4pm, recommended to ring beforehand | Tip If you prefer fun and games to war games, the museum also holds seaside memorabilia for a skip down memory lane.

64__Downs Park

Where Duchamp's eyes opened

Contained within a landscape of residential streets remains a rare reminder of a key landmark referencing 20th-century artist Marcel Duchamp. The playful French master spent time in Herne Bay during a balmy 1913 summer. He played tennis at the town courts, now gone, but it was on Downs Park that he accompanied his sister, Yvonne, who attended language classes at Lynton College on this quiet road, not far from the curve of the grassy Downs overlooking the sea. Although the English language school no longer exists, the building remains.

Herne Bay and its distinctive residential and seaside architecture gave the conceptualist plenty to think about. The double-pane format of one of his works, *The Large Glass*, is thought to echo the proportions of the sash window, and he often experimented with glass during his career. Duchamp also wrote that he was 'enchanted' by the lengthy pier (see ch. 77). One of the first pieces he created when he returned to Paris was *Bicycle Wheel*, which recalls a huge, spoked wheel that made up part of the pier's entertainment offerings.

A plaque notes the artist's links to this suburban, rarely visited road lined with mature trees. But events related to Duchamp in the town are always well received. The Seaside Museum displays exhibits dedicated to the artist, and Beach Creative (see ch. 62) includes a gallery named after him. A seaside bench created by Margot Laureau and unveiled in 2014 also referenced the town's links with the artist but sadly did not survive storms. Duchamp did not spend long in the town, but he called the weather 'superb'. In a letter to painter Max Bergmann that summer, Duchamp wrote, 'I am not dead; I am in Herne Bay.'

For a surreal piece of local architecture which would have fascinated Marcel Duchamp today, head to nearby Mickleburgh Hill, on the town's edge, for the space-age, cone-topped water tower.

Address Downs Park, Herne Bay, CT6 6BY | Getting there 20-minute walk from Herne Bay station via Station Road and King's Road towards Beltinge Road | Hours Unrestricted | Tip Duchamp's *Fountain* is considered a 20th-century masterpiece. The Victorian Portland stone fountain at Waltrop Gardens may not have commanded such attention but is still worth observing.

65 Boy with a Boat

Our boy gazes at the horizon

Perched on a wall not far from the historic pier (see ch. 77) is this sculpture of a boy who may have eaten too many ice creams, such is his chubbiness. Carved out of Portland limestone by London-based artist Paula Haughney, the boy clutches a boat in his arms and looks out at sea. He has been there for ever, hasn't he, with his intense and dreamy gaze?

Well, no. Back in the early 1990s the sculptor made many models of this little cherub before exhibiting them at the then Macari's (now Makcari's) restaurant, with customers voting this one their favourite. It's easy to see why. He's a lost soul but his boat grounds him and reminds us of our childhood toys. When asked if the boy's affections for his boat are a nod to the heritage of Herne Bay's colourful, steamboat past, Haughney's response rather recalls *Citizen Kane*: 'It had arisen more from me having a toy boat as a child to which my mother attached a string so it wouldn't be lost.' She adds: 'The boy is holding his boat as he is reluctant to let it go.'

Sourced in Dorset, the stone was cut in two for the sculpture. When quizzed about the boy's many-times-larger-than-life-sized heft, Haughney explains: 'I usually go down the quarry to choose my stone but I was pregnant at the time so they sent me the stone unseen. It was bigger than I asked for but I carved it anyway.' Unveiled by Herne Bay native and ex-*EastEnders'* actor John Altman, the boy is a much-loved piece of the seafront landscape. It captured imaginations so much that it won the Rouse award for public sculptures when public art was not so widely discussed.

Although it does not scream of its presence, this subtle piece suits the town. Unfortunately, the sculpture has not just attracted fans of its peaceful visage but also the attention of vandals in the past who have drawn on and defaced the boy. Best send Nasty Nick to sort them out.

Address Sea wall, Central Parade, Herne Bay, CT6 5JN | Getting there From Herne Bay station, 12-minute walk down Station Road to Central Parade; Central Parade car park | Hours Unrestricted | Tip The sweet dancing couple sculpture in Mortimer Street is also worth a look.

66 Brides in the Bath Site

Come on in – the water's lovely

Behind this standard shopfront, originally number 80 before the High Street reorganisation of the 1930s, lies a morbid history. In 1912, George Joseph Smith, the son of an insurance clerk, brought his new bride to Herne Bay and to this address. But poor Bessie Mundy was not due to start a life of wedded bliss but to serve as a victim. Smith, who went by many aliases, was a serial bigamist who had plundered his previous wives for their savings. Here, he went one step further. After installing a bath in their short-lived marital home, Smith (whom Bessie knew as Williams) took his wife to a local doctor, claiming she was suffering epileptic fits (Smith had convinced her she had no memory of them). A day before the doctor was to make a home visit, Smith pulled Bessie under the bathwater by her ankles, forcing water into her nose and mouth, and drowning her.

Before her death, the couple had drawn up mutual wills, so Smith was able to disappear to the north of England with a £2,500 inheritance in his hand. Emboldened by his earnings – worth some £290,000 in 2020 – Smith carried out the same audacious stunt on two more unsuspecting women. Both Alice Burnham and Margaret Lofty died in a similar style, and he secured their legacies without raising significant concern.

Because Margaret Lofty died in London and not a seaside town, the news became national, and the father of Alice Burnham read about it in the *News of the World*. When he notified the police of the coincidence, the bodies of all three women were exhumed and re-examined by a pathologist. The findings led to enhanced subsequent legal proceedings as it was discovered that his crimes followed a pattern. This was later referred to as 'system' in legal terms. Smith was tried at the Old Bailey in London, and after jury deliberations of just 20 minutes, was sentenced to death in Kent's Maidstone prison in 1915.

Address 159 High Street, CT6 5AQ | Getting there 12-minute walk from Herne Bay station through Memorial Park and crossing Mortimer Street; Market Street parking | Hours Exterior unrestricted | Tip For a traditional ironmonger like the one George Smith bought his bath from, or more modern DIY essentials, head to Baydis at 7 William Street.

67 __ Briggsy's
Ready for your close-up?

In a town born to trade in antiques and house clearances, such is the abundance of retirees, Briggsy's Antiques Emporium takes the second-hand crown. With several floors of treasures such as porcelain snowmen, bevelled mirrors, vintage movie posters, silk kimonos and models of classic cars, it's hard not to be overwhelmed by the sheer volume and higgledy-piggledy range of goods you can haggle over. Wriggle through the maze and lose yourself to a throbbing 1950s and 1960s soundtrack!

But if you think the contents of this emporium are interesting, wait till you hear the story behind the building itself. The only purpose-built building for entertainment in the town centre other than pubs, it was constructed in 1899 in a neoclassical style, and named the Washington Arcade before changing its name to the Cinema De Luxe in 1911. After a few more re-names and a period as part of the Union Cinema chain, it was finally closed as a cinema in 1937. In a strange switcheroo, it became a clothing factory for a spell, before settling down as Briggsy's in 2008.

There are other more fashionable places in town to kit out your beachfront property, but this one is unforgettable for its variety and size, billing itself as the largest place in Herne Bay for furniture. If you want something to spice up your home, large or small, you will most probably find it here and half the fun is found in looking for it. It is still clear that this was once a cinema and the word 'Pictures' is etched on the stonework of the entrance beneath a feature tower and distinctive domed roof.

Inside, the cavernous size and original elements and plaster decoration of the cinema to the rear won't let you forget that the building once offered a very different type of entertainment. Despite its current incarnation, it is not hard to picture the glory of Saturday mornings thrilling to westerns and comedies.

Address 75 High Street, CT6 5LQ, +44 (0)1227 370621 | Getting there 12-minute walk from Herne Bay station via Station Road turning right onto the High Street; Market Street car park | Hours Tue–Sat 10am–4pm | Tip Herne Bay is no stranger to the director's gaze with legendary 1970s show *Upstairs Downstairs* shot in the town as well as BBC's *Little Britain* making use of the clock tower and Central Parade as a backdrop for several sketches.

68__ Central Bandstand
Escape the tides of time

The perfect location of this traditional local meeting point was once its downfall, with it suffering many drenches from the sea. The devastating North Sea flood of 1953 left the Central Bandstand badly damaged but today it has been restored and is now as graceful as it when it first opened in 1924. The original section incorporated two sea-facing balconies with space for deckchairs. Forward-thinking architects did plan for the coastal winds, if not for the seas, with metal and glazed sliding screens at the east and west of the building. These could be drawn out across the promenade when a band was playing and retracted when the music ended. The frontage added in 1932 was built of steel, cast iron, glass and teak and gave the largely reinforced concrete structure extra Art Deco flair. Herne Bay's popularity meant that by the late 1920s it was joined by other bandstands such as one at the King's Hall and another one on the Downs. The popularity of this one meant that audiences for the military brass bands began to spread across to Tower Gardens and spilled out onto the road.

During World War II the pier (see ch. 77) was deployed for military needs, and the bandstand was proposed as a shelter, but reputedly earned the nickname of 'Adolf's Bath House' because at high tide the restless seas would flood the place. Instead, anglers were allowed to fish from the rooftop balcony.

Architectural drawings made during its 1932 revamp did include a full roof covering but this never materialised and bar the stage it is still exposed to the elements. By the 1970s it was disused and damaged, but with some determined efforts from locals and English Heritage, the building, including its distinctive cupolas, was restored in 1998–1999 and it's possible to view the sea from the cafe inside it. For anyone craving some pre-war glamour, glide up its elegant steps and step back in time.

Address Central Parade, CT6 5JN | **Getting there** 15-minute walk via Station Road and then right at Central Parade; Central Parade car park | **Hours** Exterior unrestricted, interior closes at dusk | **Tip** Greensted's Café on William Street's awnings may be modern but look a little closer at the façade's faded clues to its former incarnation as a master butcher's.

69 __ Clock Tower

Lights, clock, action!

This Grade II listed clock, one of the oldest of its kind in the world, is impossible to miss. Built thanks to generous and eccentric benefactress and Herne Bay fan, Ann Thwaytes, it jolts into view as you make your way to the coast. When the tower was built in 1837 its primary function was to tell the time; now, thanks to modern technology, it also tells the tide. Fitting as it is so close to the sea.

Renovations by lighting experts saw it tricked up with LED lights which change colour according to the whims of the often-unpredictable waves. At low tide, the top section glows in vibrant response to whatever the waves are up to, a feat made possible by exciting technology and the might of extensive tidal data. But even without this illumination, there is still beauty in its graceful Portland stone. Referencing the style of a Grecian temple it is an unlikely addition to the predominantly Victorian seafront architectural landscape. Created by a local craftsman, and listed as Grade II in 1951, the clock retains the architectural style of the past despite the funding it has received and the technology livening it up. Said to be some 77 feet tall, it towers above the skyline and is crowned by a weathervane. Look out for the cannons on either side of the tower, which were dredged from the sea when the town's third pier was being created.

A memorial plaque was added as a tribute to the 36 men from Herne Bay and the surrounding areas who served time in the Second Boer War. It is a respectful list of those who volunteered so much during the South African conflict that attracts scant attention today. But it is above all the clock that turns heads, and it is one of the traditional symbols of Herne Bay. Whether or not it can claim to be the first freestanding tidal clock in the world is a matter of debate, but it is most probably the oldest purpose-built, freestanding clock tower to change with the tides. Next time you view this impressive structure why not gaze at it and take into account its wonderful history?

Address 72 Central Parade, CT6 5JQ | Getting there 15-minute walk from Herne Bay station via Station Road heading towards the coast; Central Parade car park | Hours Unrestricted | Tip Herne Bay's seafront gardens features a sundial gifted to the town by the burgermeister of the German town of Waltrop.

70 __ East Cliff Shelter

A quiet resting place … again

An 1889 report in *Herne Bay Illustrated* includes a sketch of a new shelter proposed for the East Cliff segment of the promenade. It was designed by Londoner J. R. Withers and took its place facing the sea after being supported by local volunteers and a generous benefactor.

According to the article, the shelter was proposed to be a 'quiet resting place' for people to admire the gorse-fringed sea views or listen to the military music from the seaside bandstands, 'While those who are of an entomological turn of mind … can indulge their bent by capturing for their home cabinets specimens of various butterflies and other lepidoptera.' Unpalatable today, mounting butterflies by killing them, setting them and pinning them in cases was a popular Victorian pastime. The article is prophetic, noting that the town will expand, but the author is sure that Herne Bay's 'openness' and 'great charm' will be enhanced by these shelters. Many of Herne Bay's other original late-Victorian shelters are still standing. The Japanese influences popular at the time can be seen in many of the iron brackets holding up their roofs.

Although shelters such as this one are loved for their unique designs, they also attract vandalism. This was the fate of the original shelter which was burned to the ground. Herne Bay volunteers came to the rescue again and they campaigned for the council to construct a new shelter. The attractive white 2019 version is the one on this stretch now. It is in a slightly different, more open location from the original shelter in an attempt to reduce the vandalism risk.

Today's East Cliff Shelter offers access for wheelchair users and pushchairs and has been designed to mitigate water damage in an area which has previously experienced devestating floods. After resting here, why not stroll towards one of the town's Victorian-style metallic blue seaside telescopes for clear views of the sea?

Address Beacon Hill, The Downs | Getting there 15-minute walk from Herne Bay station through Memorial Park, then towards the sea and along the promenade towards Reculver; Reculver car park | Hours Unrestricted | Tip St George's toilets at Central Parade were once part of a bath house complex that included a grand seaside shelter. The complex fell out of use by the 1900s, but the original ceramic toilets are still in working order.

71__Famous
of Herne Bay Mural

Count them if you can

As if looking down from heaven, this rather dreamlike mural high above the crazy golf course shows off the great names associated with the town. English-born American comedian Bob Hope presides over the montage, and he is probably the most famous name on it, even though his connection with the town is literally tenuous. He once fell off the pier, and the world could easily have been deprived of Bing Crosby's movie partner, such is the severity of a drop from the structure.

Less dramatic is the sight of cheeky Ken Russell, who brought his customary frisson to the town in the 1960s, shooting sex comedy *French Dressing* between the King's Hall and the pebbly stretch of beach. The auteur even went onto to describe Herne Bay as the finest place he had ever been. Other notable people joining the party include quizmaster of ITV's *Blockbusters* and favourite of Generation X, Bob Holness. Although born in South Africa the affable presenter of the much-loved game show described the town as 'A terrific place for me . . . it had its own beach and Mortimer Street was always busy and bustling.'

Other famous faces include actor John Altman, frequently booed and hissed at for his infamous portrayal of 'Nasty' Nick Cotton in long-running BBC soap *EastEnders*. Joining him is modish 1960s pop-star Peter Noone of cheery hitmakers Herman's Hermits, who at the height of his success bought his parents a 20-bedroomed hotel in the town. At the other end of the musical spectrum is the angelic-looking psychedelic rock star Kevin Ayers with the devilish taste for excess.

Created by Kent-based artist Penny Bearman, who has made some other murals in Herne Bay including a seaside postcard-style mural you have to crane your neck to take in, this one is by far the most entertaining in its daubed celebration of this small town's cultural contribution to the world.

Address 141 Central Parade, CT6 8SS | Getting there From the station walk down Pier Avenue and then onto Central Parade; Central Parade car park | Hours Unrestricted | Tip The amusement arcades nearby are the place to spend small and dream big.

72__Golding Surplus

Fashion that is not rationed

This part of the world has been key to defence in England for decades. Regiments fired out on the coast and the pier (see ch. 77)
for military purposes during World War I. Zeppelins and Gothas
bombed the town with locals fleeing for safety to the King's Hall
(see ch. 78) during World War II. So, a khaki-green, flag-draped,
army surplus shop at the cusp of the town's shopping parade seems
perfectly logical. Step back into wartime without the danger in this
expansive space dominated by rails of new-issue and army surplus
wear. With items dating back to World War II, this shop, open
since 2000 and with another branch in Canterbury, has an artillery
of war-related goods.

When Paul and Melanie Golding (still at the helm) started this
enterprise, they would take the stock sourced from the UK, Germany and France to places like nearby Folkestone in a borrowed
Ford Fiesta. They have sold their camouflage wear and khaki jackets
at major festivals like Glastonbury and Reading, as well as at the Military Odyssey in Kent, which overflows with wartime memorabilia.

Their clientele ranges from the ex-army types who like to rem-
inisce to those preparing for a weekend's camping. You can grab
a hip flask here for whisky on the go as well as chunky boots and
Soviet Bloc-era gas masks. You'll find all sorts of air guns here, as
well as NATO-issued brass bullets, which make unusual paper-
weights. There are also less-disarming goods, such as British Army
surplus metal containers, which are a unique and handy form of
storage. Pale-blue vintage mess tins from the US Army join *Top
Gun*-style aviator sunglasses, but its roots are in the town. Whether
it is its long local history, the cascade of glittery medals behind
the counter highlighting Kentish bravery and sacrifice, or just the
affection in which the store is held, Golding Surplus wins both the
war and the peace.

Address 169 Mortimer Street, CT6 5HE, +44 (0)1227 749141, www.goldingsurplus.co.uk, paul@goldingsurplus.co.uk | Getting there 15-minute walk from Herne Bay station via Memorial Park and Beach Street; Market Street car park | Hours Mon, Wed, Fri & Sat 9.30am–5pm | Tip Marine Hotel at nearby Tankerton was a former military hospital during World War II and the framed prints of Whitstable on its walls draw attention to the region's past (www.marinewhitstable.co.uk).

73_ The Hampton Inn

Rough tides inspire Ripper detective

Where's Hampton-on-Sea? You're in it – or rather, you're in its one remaining intact building. Once a village sitting between Herne Bay and Whitstable, devastating erosion means there is little reminder of what it once was. Sip an ale in this pub, formerly The Hampton Pier Inn, and ponder the lives lived in the now drowned fishing hamlet.

In the 1860s the Herne Bay, Hampton and Reculver Oyster Fishery Company was founded here, with the marine environment key to its plans. The company constructed a 300-metre-long pier and terraced homes for workers, but the venture was eventually unsuccessful. Then, in 1879, the owner of the *Herne Bay Argus*, Thomas Freeman, dreamed up a seaside residential estate on the land including a bandstand, golf course and archery green, and he even sold shares in it. But Freeman died shortly before his vision could take off. With the pier causing eddies, interfering with the natural movement of the replenishing nature of the beach shingle, the coastline was left vulnerable, and it began to swiftly erode. By 1897 the already wary residents had their worst fears realised when the 'Great Storm' took its toll.

As the residents were left pondering their fate, an unofficial champion named Edmund Reid took note. The former detective was already well known for his handling of the notorious London Jack the Ripper murders which remain unsolved today. Despite campaigning enthusiastically – and eccentrically, such as establishing the settlement's hotel (his shed), he was also unsuccessful here. His dreams of development died, and the tides turned for good in 1921 when the village vanished under water, and the community faded away leaving only this pub and a few fragments of pier. Oysters have now returned to being big business along this coastline and the metal trestle tables visible from Reeves Beach (see ch. 101) are key to cultivating non-native species.

Address 72 Western Esplanade, Hampton-on-Sea, CT6 8DL, +44 (0)1227 362216, www.hamptoninnhernebay.co.uk | **Getting there** 20-minute walk from Herne Bay station in the direction of Whitstable; bus 919 from Herne Bay station; Hampton Pier car park | **Hours** Mon–Thu 11am–10pm, Fri & Sat 11am–11pm, Sun noon–9.30pm | **Tip** Edmund Reid is buried in Herne Bay's Victorian cemetery, as are several members of the artistic Dalziel family, including a brother who reproduced several of John Tenniel's illustrations for *Alice in Wonderland* for print.

74 __ Herne Village
Murder and the high seas

The village of Herne is full of the vestiges of its past position as a haven for smugglers. Not that there weren't government officials watching out for it, as well as a coastal blockade trying to thwart it. Revenue officers monitored the hazardous shipping channels, both on land and on sea.

But smugglers have always found their way. For example, look up at the chimneys of some of Herne's Grade II listed cottages and you'll discover a triangular adjoining spyhole. These provide access to view the road leading to the coast, so smugglers could see if the road was clear, without being seen. Locals (and some officials) would often turn a blind eye to smuggling, especially as it provided hard-to-source goods. Millers were willing to turn their windmill sails (known as sweeps) to warn smugglers not to come ashore whenever officers were about. Standing atop a hill, Herne Mill, at three storeys high, is so prominent it can be seen from the Thanet Way. This rare and well-preserved example of the Kentish smock mill was once used as a 'sea mark' (navigational landmark for shipping) on the Thames Estuary.

Herne's thriving Smugglers Inn was a popular haunt of the North Kent gang. They and their rival gangs dealt in whisky, tea, lace and gin. One morning in 1821, a group of blockade men came upon them bringing their goods to shore, in front of The Ship (see ch. 85). In an exchange of fire, during which his gun misfired, Midshipman Sydenham Snow was killed. Despite overwhelming evidence, no one was convicted of Snow's brutal murder. His grave can be found in Herne's St Martin's churchyard, where some of the corpses were buried wrapped in the smuggler's favourite – sheep's wool. Because the 18th-century trade of fine English wool was subject to strict export rules, it could be smuggled for a profit, referred to as 'owling'. Sheppey, off the coast, means Island of Sheep.

Address CT6 7AN | Getting there 1-mile by car or taxi from Herne Bay | Hours Exterior unrestricted | Tip The volunteers at the National Coastwatch Institution keep watch over Herne Bay's seas in a converted Victorian toilet block on Herne Bay's sea front. The white building is still referred to as The Old Bathing Station.

75 Herne Bay Little Theatre
No small drama

Unusually for a theatre, this one, the smallest in the area, is to be found on a quiet residential street lined with quince trees. It's so modest as to be difficult to find, but a lack of size (just 72 seats) does not translate into a lack of ambition, with Dennis Potter adaptions being performed alongside the Noel Coward classics.

Herne Bay was a very different place when the theatre opened in 1987, until which time keen theatre fans could only rely on the King's Hall for entertainment. This theatre came to the rescue with its roots in amateur productions and ad hoc funding. Although it cannot compete with starrier examples in Canterbury, there is something enchanting abouts this place, its friendly staff and volunteerism.

The building was once a Catholic order, and the nuns worshipping here used this base for seaside breaks for city children from the capital. It has passed through several other incarnations, but it has maintained its rather hallowed atmosphere, with its reverential darkness and quietness outside of showtimes. Alive and bold during a showing, pantomimes draw in the crowds and the regular film night is hard to beat. You can always grab a drink or some ice cream at the interval and the shows change regularly. You could do no worse than a night out in this old-fashioned and lovingly maintained theatre with its expressive sets. It captures the essence of comedy, drama and history on its intimate stage. As for *Jeeves and Wooster* (Jeeves visited Herne Bay in his comic novels) the staff admit they do not regularly perform PG Wodehouse adaptations. Missing a trick? Maybe. But Philip Robinson, secretary of the theatre, assures me that they are doing fine without the PG Wodehouse connection – their productions nearly always sell out, he says with a grin. And with the prices as petite as its size, it would be difficult not to.

Address 44 Buller's Avenue, CT6 8UH, +44 (0)1227 366004, www.hernebaylittletheatre.com, info@hernebaylittletheatre.co.uk | Getting there 5-minute walk from Herne Bay station; very limited parking | Hours Exterior unrestricted; see website for production updates | Tip If you're visiting in the warmest months, Strode Park in nearby Herne has an amphitheatre for summer productions.

76—Herne Bay Mini Golf
You'll swing for this one

Can't get out and practise your swing? Never mind, mini golf is in Herne Bay, just beyond the amusement arcade strip and beneath an eye-catching mural (see ch. 71). A round of its tiny, green course can be completed in under an hour depending on your competitive spirit. Eighteen holes amongst some well-placed obstacles provide seaside fun, and it is floodlit at dusk. For the uninitiated, mini golf is regular golf minus the great distances and the great swinging strokes, plus a bit of whimsy. The aim of putting the ball across a surface to enter the hole is key.

Also popular in the United States (where it is sometimes referred to as 'putt-putt'), Sweden and Germany, mini golf is a fixture of many English seaside towns. It does not require membership fees or expensive equipment, or even large amounts of practice. The pastime boomed in the UK during the 1970s and was hugely popular at coastal resorts at a time when travelling abroad would not have been economically possible for many. Despite the boom in package holidays, it is still a popular pastime today.

Mini golf (like fun and crazy golf, which also feature in many English coastal towns, plus pitch and putt) straddles generations, sexes and classes, but independent courses are in danger of being drowned out by the big players. Yet this artificial-turfed course with its tricky obstacles, potted palms and fun murals is as beloved to Herne Bay as a Makcari's ice cream (see ch. 79). Established in 2006, it is within putting distance of the pier (see ch. 77), and the whirr of the amusement arcades nearby add to the seaside reverie. It is uncovered, but keen mini golfers such as those who enter national championships battle on despite the rain.

But even if this course is beyond you, you can just sit and watch others perfect their Lilliputian bounce with a sugary doughnut from the café right beside it.

Address 141 Central Parade, CT6 8SS, +44 (0)1227 375098, www.ifunatsandancers.co.uk, enquiries@ifun.co.uk | Getting there 15-minute walk from Herne Bay station via Station Road heading towards the sea then left at Central Parade; Neptune car park | Hours Daily 10am–5pm | Tip Bingo is another classic seaside activity and it can be played whatever the weather. Connaught Bingo & Social Club on Central Parade is not tied to any of the big players, which makes it a rarity.

77__Herne Bay Pier

Steam ahead on a traditional pier

There's something very special about a British seaside pier, especially now as so many resorts have lost theirs. But Herne Bay is not a quitter – its pier is now on its third incarnation. The first began glamorously, thanks to its official designer, the legendary engineer Thomas Telford, also famous for his canals. Telford's three-quarter-mile-long wooden pier was opened in 1831 to capture the paddle steamer holiday market for the town. Passengers arriving from both London and nearby Thanet were delighted to arrive in the bustling seaside town, with more than 30,000 people said to have landed in 1835, and over 40,000 in 1842. Sadly, damage from hungry shipworms and winter storms did for Telford's pier, so a second one was built in 1873, using cast iron and featuring a theatre and shops. Then the third pier was built in 1899 to accommodate the town's rising popularity especially amongst visitors from London and Essex. Encased in barbed wire during World War II due to invasion fears, it reopened after the war, but damage from storms and frozen seas led to its abandonment. You can't keep a good pier down though, and since 2008 the Herne Bay Pier Trust has been dedicated to bringing it back to life.

Their efforts have been successful. Clever use of pastel beach huts makes the most of the space, selling all sorts, with food from classic British grub to Thai cuisine. Further down the pier, a merry-go-round and helter-skelter lend a fairground touch. There is a certain spooky charm about the abandoned remains of the stump of the derelict pierhead further out, but there are even talks about bringing that into use too. One suggestion is to reconnect it and install renewable energy technology. For now, though, it remains at sea, resisting demolition and hinting at the time when it was such a long pier it even had its own railway transport running from ship to shore.

Address 81 Central Parade, CT6 5JN | Getting there 15-minute walk from Herne Bay station down Station Road and then Central Parade; Neptune car park | Hours Unrestricted | Tip Near the entrance of the pier is a memorial with details of the time in 1945 when H. J. Wilson flew a record 606.25 mph in a gold yellow Gloster Meteor F4 between East Cliffs and Reculver Towers.

78_King's Hall
A history of entertainment

This hall has captivated concertgoers with its original Edwardian features and beach views for years. Opened first in 1904 and named the East Cliff Hall, and then again in its second incarnation in 1913, it stands somewhat lonely on the stretch towards Reculver called the Downs. Originally a bandstand, it was funded by a Thomas Dence, who specified no 'beach minstrels' and no 'conjurors or variety entertainments' either.

There were many architectural specifications to cope with the threat of subsidence and coastal battering, and so far it has weathered these threats well. Inside it is glamorous with favourable acoustics and a maple dance floor. The King's Hall has offered a wide, welcoming place for entertainment, offering seating for 1,500 people. In its heyday, audience members sank back in tip-up chairs of green plush and lights shimmered above. Unveiled by the Princess Beatrice, the medallion plaque of Edward VIII inside was carved by high society artist Emil Fuchs. Thought to be a highly lifelike portrait of the King, it was fashioned from marble.

The venue adapted to the changing times. During World War II, when Herne Bay was a particularly popular location for Nazi bombers and Kent was referred to as 'Hellfire County' due to its position as a frontier region and defender of London, The King's Hall was where local residents were fitted for their gas masks. Bewildered children would have been fitted with Mickey Mouse masks as they sheltered here. Now, the venue trades in tribute bands and nostalgia acts, but it once welcomed military bands as well as opera. Professional wrestling had a period of popularity too – we wonder what high-brow Dence would have thought of this. If you are not looking to attend a night out, it has a café open in the day with seating outside to enjoy the view. Sometimes it features visual art from local talent in the foyer.

Address Beacon Hill, CT6 6BA, +44 (0)1227 374188, www.thekingshall.com | Getting there 15-minute walk from Herne Bay station via the High Street and onto King's Road, along the coast towards Reculver; Neptune car park | Hours Café: daily 10am-3pm; check website for event schedule | Tip For live entertainment in a cosy setting, the Divers Arms on the Central Parade has music nights every Friday and Saturday (www.diversarms.co.uk).

79___Makcari's

The nicest ices, retro style

Since the 1930s, Makcari's has taken corner stage on Herne Bay's genteel seafront and has been serving up ice creams ranging from the divine to the garish. Hand-made gelato flavours include Ferrero Rocher, Baileys and Turkish Delight, and they are sweet and silky as they melt on the tongue. Joining these lately have been developments such as Marmite-flavoured ices, and not at a Heston Blumenthal price either. The cakes here are also inviting and come in portions that would scare competitive eaters. If you fancy healthier options, there are also gluten-free versions and other varieties bringing you straight back to the 21st century.

But who is Makcari's trying to kid? This place is like something out of *Mad Men* with wine-coloured banquettes, hanging bulbs and huge windows for looking out onto the coast whilst you ponder the world over a mug of tea. Malt vinegar, sadly missing from so many dining establishments these days, joins the condiments on the Formica tables. There is no fancy salt here either. But if you just want to sit on a bench with a dreamy creamy ice then the parlour will let you do that without going inside. Other goodies to help you revitalize on your seaside trip include fluffy oven-baked jacket potatoes, crispy waffles and crepes, plus cream teas oozing jam. Coffee is cheap and frothily delightful. For those chasing a more saccharine hit, Makcari's has boldly deemed itself 'The World's First Hot Chocolate Bar'. This may be debatable, but you can nevertheless indulge in a cup of hot chocolate with a bewildering variety of flavours such as macadamia and coconut.

There is another Makcari's spot inside Central Bandstand (see ch. 68) which is good for pizza and wraps, but this one is the place to go for a traditional seaside dinner of fish and chips in a setting that takes you straight back into another era. It's an expansive space so you'll be able to settle down and enjoy each other's company without feeling cramped.

Address 54 Central Parade, CT6 5JG, +44 (0)1227 374977, www.makcaris.com,
nejmi.hassan@sky.com | Getting there 12-minute walk from Herne Bay station towards
Mortimer Street and then toward the sea; Central Parade car park | Hours Summer
Mon–Thu 8am–8pm, Fri–Sun 8am–9pm; winter Mon–Thu 8am–6pm, Fri–Sun
8am–7pm | Tip Revival Ice Cream Parlour and Veggie Vinyl Eatery in Whitstable is a
colourful place with many vegan and gluten-free icy treats, and is socially responsible as well,
working closely with mental health charity Mind (www.revivalwhitstable.co.uk).

80 Memorial Park

Forget Me Not

The Great War was not just something that Herne Bay residents of the time read about in the newspapers. They could often hear the noise of the heavy gunfire drifting across the Channel from nearby Flanders, and also had to contend with the barbed wire and defence force of regiments along the coast. Celebrations began when the conflict ended in 1918, but the need for a permanent memorial was paramount. Surrounded by flame-red poppies and hardy greenery in the middle of the Memorial Park, this stark obelisk flanked by steps was unveiled in 1922 and serves as a monument to those who lost their lives in this war and, later, others. Although a little neglected, it remains striking at the apex of a tree-lined avenue of remembrance, within a grassy expanse often filled with people walking dogs and relaxing.

Locals have always been amongst the bravest around. The family of Herne Bay-native Harry Wells received a Victoria Cross to mark his sacrifice and were present to plant a tree in his memory on the centenary of the end of the conflict in 2018. Others fallen in 20th-century wars are also remembered in black lettering on smooth panels. These include those who died in conflicts such as the Falklands War and the Iraq War.

If you'd rather just relax than observe history, the park also offers tennis courts, a bowling green, a boating lake and a children's play area. The layout is also worth navigating as it deploys a landscape architecture referred to as 'desire lines', where trees lead the way along pedestrian pathways connecting the train station with the east of the town centre.

Elsewhere in Herne Bay you can find less-official remnants of other conflicts, such as the stumps of iron where pre-World War II garden railings used to be. But it is primarily here that World War I is remembered for changing history irrevocably and establishing our current world.

Address Pier Chine, CT6 5QH | Getting there 3-minute walk from Herne Bay station turning right onto Station Road; William Street car park | Hours Unrestricted | Tip Find more evocations of wartime in the Vintage Empire Tearoom on Herne Bay High Street, which chimes to a 1940s soundtrack and serves enemy-defeating doorstep sandwiches to boot.

81 Mustard Interiors

This place cuts the mustard

When you come to Herne Bay, you already feel like you've travelled back in time thanks to its independent shops and cafés, such as Mascot Bakery, which sells frog-shaped cakes and other sweet treats that would excite retro snapper Martin Parr, and its vivid crazy golf course.

If you want to take the vibe home by decking your apartment out in the finest vintage styling, you can look no further than Mustard Interiors. One of the owners, J. Clare Richards, admits she sources her stuff 'here, there and everywhere', with co-owner John Griffiths particularly proud of the circus panels and French mirrors. It's a small shop off the main thoroughfare of the town and due to be blended with a café, but what it lacks in size it makes up in an eclectic punch the big out-of-town chains can only dream of.

Need a vintage suitcase for all your bits and bobs? Or just fancy some botanical prints, or a slightly strange mannequin? Mustard Interiors is your place. It's slightly shabby inside and if you imagine hard enough you can see it as the former accountancy office it once housed. From bookkeepers to interiors – who said the High Street was dead?

There are so many colours here that belong to different decades, from 1960s brown to 1970s orange. It's the perfect antidote to the minimalism of the 21st century. Maximalism rules here, but you needn't spend a maximum fortune.

Kit yourself out in a Frida Kahlo necklace or pick up something unique from local artist Nina Shilling, who produces exotic prints based on Herne Bay's rich marine life. Perhaps instead you'll take a shine to a puppet – Punch and Judy shows used to thrill crowds in the Central Bandstand (see ch. 68) – or an antique cigarette box, or even an expressive taxidermied owl. If you like your living space infused with life and colour, then this place will be your heaven for your home.

Address 154 Mortimer Street, CT6 5DU, +44 (0)7597 014096 | **Getting there** 10-minute walk from Herne Bay station via Memorial Park and past Beach Street towards Central Parade; Market Street car park | **Hours** Mon–Fri 10am–4pm, Sat 9am–4pm | **Tip** The adorable animal-shaped dustbins along the promenade wouldn't look out of place in Mustard. They were ordered as an experiment, initially including voice boxes, but this expensive technology needed to be replaced quite quickly, so they are now silent.

82 Neptune's Arm

Out in the water, but not getting wet

For the next best thing to walking on water, stroll along this extended comma of bulky stone out into the bay, with the glistening sea on either side and the breath of nature on your face. A quiet spot away from the crowds on the beach, it will bring you in closer communion with the environment than walking on the pier, which can get very busy during the summer season. You can even walk at high tide, although be careful when the sea is rough.

Surrounding Neptune's Arm are boats and jet-skiers all jostling for their space in this expanse of the famously cold water. As well as the cool estuary air there is often a waft of boat engine fumes and the vinegary fragrance of chips. Taking a mere 10 minutes to walk to the end, this strong arm will take you into the heart of Herne Bay's sometimes unpredictable waters, without the hassle of renting a boat.

The defences of the north Kent coastal towns have historically come in the form of timber or stone, with the edge of vulnerable Reculver (see ch. 84) strengthened by a natural shingle mound and man-made groynes. Built in the 1990s to further bolster the existing coastal defences – including more picturesque groynes, many of which were made of tropical hardwood – Neptune's Arm has sheltered the town from the ravages of the sea, which has caused huge destruction in the past, and will hopefully protect its future. A small, chalky-blue raised platform, often blighted by graffiti, stands at the end. Climb it for wide-angle views of the town but don't forget to look at the horizon, where the sail turbines of the wind farm rotate and the lonely lump of the pier stands out, both adrift and proud. It is a popular spot for photographers and artists, and also for couples who like to use this spot for a bit of a smooch as the gulls and herons swoop. Bring your camera, your easel, or your sweetheart.

Address 55 Central Parade, CT6 5JG | Getting there 3-minute walk from Mortimer Street; Neptune car park | Hours Unrestricted | Tip This spot is also good for fishing. Try and catch bass and flounder with equipment bought from the friendly Absolute Tackle in Herne Common.

83 RAM Collectible Toys
Herne Bay's own toy story

Perhaps it is the primary-coloured, die-cast cars and miniature trains in the window. Or maybe it is the eye-catching red front. But it's difficult to pass RAM Collectible Toys without wanting to know more about this old-fashioned toy shop specialising in vintage finds for kids and big kids alike.

Action figures, posters and vehicles referencing cult series, such as *The Man from Uncle* and *The Avengers*, fill the shelves alongside rarities. 'The vintage toy shop can be as rare to find as some of the toys we sell,' explains owner Mark Priestly. And collectors, including fans from Europe, will even base their trips to Herne Bay around a visit to RAM. Younger fans also appreciate the chance to buy something unusual.

Crammed with the ultimate collectors' prize of sealed, mint treasures, the glass cabinets are an insight into popular culture of the 20th century. Finds include trains made by Hornby Hobbies, headquartered since 1964 in Margate 11 miles away. Miniature, red, double-decker buses join *Popeye* and *Bagpuss* (see ch. 2) memorabilia and comics.

Toys of the calibre and condition found here are big business. Costings at auctions and online can reach extreme figures. But what makes a toy valuable? Mark explains, 'Toys can be rare if they survived despite their fragility, or were made in small numbers, or of a subject matter no longer socially acceptable, for example.' Some toys are best left in the past, but most vintage playthings are joyful, vibrant reminders of our early lives.

Mark's enthusiasm for the shop, here since 2013, highlights the fun of discovery and of childhood memories jogged. 'Buying and selling hard-to-find toys isn't so much a job,' he says. 'It's more of a passion … the social interaction, the sharing of childhood stories … hearing the near daily exclamations of, *I had that*, or *I always wanted one of those*, is a real buzz.'

Address RAM Collectible Toys, 27 High Street, CT6 5LJ, +44 (0)7758 004824, www.ramcollectibletoys.co.uk, mark@ramcollectibletoys.co.uk | Getting there 10-minute walk from Herne Bay station down Station Road and then onto the High Street | Hours Tue – Sat 9.30am – 5.30pm | Tip Whitstable is home to several independent toy shops. Harbour Street's (see ch. 96) Buttercup, featuring wooden traditional toys and dolls, is ideal for tomorrow's collectors.

84 Reculver

From Roman stronghold to Bond lair

The writers amongst us may well think that the coastal tip of Reculver is an ideal setting for a novel. But a certain Mr Ian Fleming got there first, choosing it as a lonely haunt for arch-baddie Goldfinger.

Mystery surrounds Reculver, but historians agree that a very early Roman fort was built here – although coastal damage has destroyed many of the clues to the past. Those clues that do remain indicate that in the early part of the 3rd century the Romans chose this area for its location at one end of the now silted up Wantsum Channel. The Wantsum Channel separated the Isle of Thanet from the rest of today's Kent some 5,000 years ago, and Reculver's distinct clifftop position made it an ideal place to oversee access between the channel and the Thames estuary and keep an eye out for pirates and raiders.

By the last quarter of the 4th century, archaeological evidence suggests that the Romans had abandoned this particular part of their coastal defence network. An Anglo-Saxon monastery was constructed in 669 and the Church of St Mary was also built. It was remodelled in the 12th century to include the towers. Known here as the 'Two Sisters', the medieval towers served as navigation markers for sailors and guided ships away from choppy waters. Twin towers long before New York, these dramatic structures loom over Herne Bay and can be spied from miles around. Its remote quality also made it ideal for Barnes Wallis (see ch. 61) when it came to testing his bouncing bomb centuries later (see ch. 63). Now it's a moody jumble of walls, ruins and earthworks, and excavations have revealed the remains of children, sparking all sorts of morbid theories such as ritual Roman-era sacrifice.

It can be one of the most isolated sites in Kent. It's open all year round and free, and although it was bad for Bond it is most certainly good for us. Just don't step too close to the edge.

Address Reculver Lane, CT6 6SS | Getting there 25-minute walk from Herne Bay pier in the direction of Thanet via a steep hill and a nature park; Reculver car park | Hours Unrestricted | Tip Reculver has been a muse for scores of artists and photographers. Pencil sketches of the site, some dating back to the 1800s, are on display at The Beaney in Canterbury.

85__The Ship Inn

A watering hole for bathers and smugglers

Yes, there are many Ship Inns dotted around Kent, but this one is special as it is key to Herne Bay's development as a modern town. Oak beams abound in this Grade II listed building, one of the oldest buildings in the town, originating circa 1650.

When Herne Bay was a tiny fisherman's hamlet and beaching point for coastal trading ships, The Ship Inn, originally called The Ship (see the vibrant sign), would have stood out like a cruise ship amongst a flotilla of hoys. In the late-18th century, collier ships from Newcastle and Sunderland would offload their coal for onward transport to Canterbury by road. Then the hard-working sailors would drink the bounty of Kent – hops – here. The area surrounding the pub began to attract holidaymakers from Canterbury, with a newspaper advertisement in early 1770 boasting that a bathing machine 'the equal of any in Margate' would be available by summer, and the town began to be known as the 'healthiest watering place' in England. (Though, less wholesomely, the town – and this inn – was also a magnet for smugglers.) Through out the 1820s and 1930s, the Oxenden Estate and new town of St. Augustine began to evolve, with The Ship still at the heart, as a grid of small streets sprang up behind it. Soon there was enough custom for a post office, a bakery, and even an assembly room.

Today, the pub remains bustling and friendly. The fish and chips may not be the healthiest in England but could be considered the tastiest. Sharing many of the high-quality specifications of historic Herne Bay pubs, The Ship's status as a focus point remains unchallenged. An outdoor area is inviting for pitching up and checking today's incoming sea traffic – now more likely to be a speedboat or jet skier rather than a smuggler or a sailor covered in coal dust. But whoever drops by for a pint, they are sure a warm and cosy welcome in a friendly and well-run place.

Address 17 Central Parade, CT6 5HT, +44 (0)1227 366636, www.shiphernebay.co.uk, info@shiphernebay.co.uk | Getting there 15-minute walk from Herne Bay station down Station Road and then onto Central Parade; parking outside the pub | Hours Daily 11am–11pm | Tip For more contemporary surroundings, The Wine Bar on Mortimer Street is a perfect place for a glass or two. Its basement is snug with varied food options sourced from local suppliers available.

86__Tele-Go-Round
You'll never want to switch channels

In glorious technicolour near the pier entrance is this eccentric addition to the Herne Bay landscape. Seeds were sown for the Tele-Go-Round when in 1966 The Rotary Club, a community-focused charitable group, came up with an idea for a mechanized float called the Magic Cave, which toured the town for both amusement and charitable purposes. Its success encouraged the club to create this static version outdoors during summer for the same reasons.

Made via resourceful crafting methods involving a washing machine pump, some plywood and a coin chute, and featuring some replica characters from BBC series *The Magic Roundabout*, the original version of Tele-Go-Round was on air, or rather, on sea in 1967. Its great popularity meant a lot of wear and tear, and it is its third incarnation that turns heads today. During a refreshment of the float in 1983, the club asked permission to use *The Muppets* characters, so popular with children of the day, but their creator, Jim Henson, refused to replicate Kermit and company, gifting the club with a recording of *The Muppets* instead. But in a distinctly plucky British move, the Rotary Club decided to go ahead and populate the float with dolls bought from the shops anyway. With more technical upgrades, and to the tune of just £150, it evolved yet again, observing newer fashions in entertainment: A *Thomas the Tank Engine* puppet was unveiled and stayed until 1987.

That's not to say the *Muppets* have been replaced – Miss Piggy underwent a makeover, rendering her even more beautiful than ever. And four of the original *Magic Roundabout* puppets (including the unforgettable Zebedee) are still springing up from this jack-in-the-box style machine. With the coins still pouring in, the Tele-Go-Round is estimated to have raised over £90,000 for local charities since inception. Even Statler and Waldorf would be impressed by this one. Well, maybe.

Address 81 Central Parade, CT6 5JN | Getting there 15-minute walk from Herne Bay station down Station Road and then onto Central Parade towards the sea; Neptune car park | Hours Summer months only | Tip Dollies Corner at Beltinge is not named after childhood toys but the former owner who used to run the popular tea rooms from its thatched buildings.

87 Barcham Sewing Machinery

Sew good at this much-loved place

Vintage and modern Singer machines, 1970s signs and colourful spools of thread fill this crammed shop at the coastal tip of Harbour Street (see ch. 96). Unique even amongst this town's idiosyncratic shops, its success is due to many factors including the dedication of the owners. In the workshop on the premises, the craftsmen undertake commissions from local professionals and hobbyists, from the London Sewing Machine Museum, and even from European clients.

With roots in London's East End rag trade reaching back to 1946, the Barcham family is keeping tradition alive. It all started with John Barcham Senior, who offered an industrial sewing machine hire service to workers in the capital and nearby Essex. But like many Londoners, Barcham was a keen fan of Whitstable and its marine culture, joining the local sailing club here and in Tankerton. In 1975 he took the leap to settle in the town and established this blue-fronted shop. Offering his crafting talents to his beloved Whitstable Yacht Club (see ch. 110) was a next, natural step.

Today his sons, John and Fred, carry on the tradition by creating sails for the club in hardy, UV-resistant, densely woven terylene using an industrial zigzag sewing machine, and the shop repairs machines strong enough to stitch marquees and leather goods. They also sharpen household knives, garden tools and scissors, but sewing machines and haberdashery are the main focus.

As this is Whitstable, local sewers don't always conform to the craft's cosy image. Since 2016, Whitstable's Profanity Embroidery Group have attracted attention for their creations embroidered with choice cuss words. The all-female group meets regularly at the Duke of Cumberland pub, and their explicit works have been displayed at Oxford Street's Fishslab Gallery and the Whitstable Biennale.

Address 59 Harbour Street, CT5 1AG, + 44 (0)1227 264271, www.barcham-sewing.co.uk |
Getting there 12-minute walk from Whitstable station via Station Road and then turning
into Oxford Street before Harbour Street, Harbour car park | Hours Mon–Sat 9am–5pm |
Tip Residential Regent's Street is home to a leading member of the Profanity Group who
dusted down a skip find for her front window. Known locally as the 'Whitstable Jesus' this
mannequin messiah features (non-sweary) messages that change regularly.

88 The Beacon House
Over the seven seas

Looking more like something out of a New England painting than a Kentish seaside is The Beacon House. Built in the early 20th century high above the natural promontory that is The Street, the house, with its pastel colours and broad veranda, bridges the gap between Whitstable and the less-visited Tankerton.

Just how did Atlantic maritime-style architecture end up in this part of Kent? Hardy Whitstable sailors, who had travelled to Canada in 1906, returned with the felled timber, which they used to build this house. Inside, white, tongue-and-groove panelling references the simplicity and functionality of the Shaker style. An Arts and Crafts sitting room reflects the more decorative trend in vogue between about 1880 and 1920. The house and its special elements have been featured in *The New York Times* and in a Saturdays' pop music video.

The Beacon House's ample qualities have not been lost on local literary talent either. Detective Pearl Nolan, in the well-loved novels by Whitstable-based author Julie Washer, loves the place, which was also featured in the television adaptation. In Pearl's own words, 'Although there were grander, more expensive seaside homes, especially along the western coast of Seasalter … Beacon House boasted a more distinctive style and, arguably, the best sea view in Whitstable.'

But The Beacon House is not simply an attractive building. Its name refers to the beacon that once stood in its garden, warning fisherfolk of potential hazards. Today, the timber groynes that divide the beach into picturesque sections provide sturdy tidal defence. The shingle beaches at Whitstable and Tankerton act as a naturally occurring buffer to the sea's strong easterly winds. And the concrete floor of Whitstable's working harbour provides yet more armour to protect locals from the worst ravages of the roaring sea.

Address The Beacon House, Tankerton Beach, CT5 2BS, + (0) 44 7813 642525, www.thebeaconhouse.co.uk, emily@thebeaconhouse.co.uk | Getting there 20-minute walk from Whitstable station down Cromwell Road and onto Harbour Street, past the harbour toward Tankerton | Hours Unrestricted from the outside; contact to book an overnight stay | Tip East of Tankerton is the Long Rock headland. An important coastal site for nature and wildlife, its long history occasionally reveals fragments relating to the Early Bronze Age, as well as the Middle Ages. Even elephant teeth have been discovered here.

89 Brian Haw Bench
Peace is the word

This huge bench may look distorted in the company of more con-
servative seaside benches, but it captures the poetic, passionate mind
of the man it was created to remember. Carved with peace symbols
and big enough for more than the usual number of people, it is a place
to reflect on the campaigning of peace visionary and former local
Brian Haw. Son of a wartime sniper, Haw spent his teenage years in
Whitstable, where his family were members of an evangelical church.
These were the 1960s, when the town smelled of joss sticks and was
a magnet for the students of nearby Kent University rejecting the
more traditionally minded Canterbury, as well as others who sought
a different way of life.

Several decades later, Haw waged a one-man protest in Parliament
Square outside Westminster against the West's sanctions against Iraq,
persisting for nearly 10 years, through fractious weather and many
attempts to evict him. Although he did not manage to bring world
peace, he certainly impacted contemporary protest.

Locals stumped up £2,000 to commemorate their committed local
hero in this enduring way, and local firm Moosejaw Woodworks
crafted it from durable oak. The unveiling of this angular but inviting
seat on International Children's Day in 2014 was accompanied by
several events in the town to celebrate Haw's life and reflect on his
legacy, and attended by artist Mark Wallinger, who won the Turner
Prize in 2007 with a faithful recreation of Haw's anti-war protest.
Although the bench looks vulnerable as it braves the elements right
on the beach, if you take the time to relax there you will feel sheltered. Haw would no doubt be glad to know that protesters now
assemble here as they gather momentum on both peace and climate
change issues.

It's a fitting spot for these meetings, as the glorious sunsets are a
reminder of nature's abundant gifts.

Address Keam's Yard, Island Wall, CT5 1AZ | **Getting there** Walk down the High Street onto Harbour Street and make your way towards the sea; Keam's Yard car park | **Hours** Unrestricted | **Tip** A few steps away is Pearson's Arms with its fruity ciders, inventive cooking and eco credentials such as encouraging its visitors to pick plastic from the beach. Brian Haw would be proud.

90_ Cold War Monitoring Post
Protect and survive?

This mottled-green, weather-battered structure could have meant the difference between life and death. Structures like these were designed to help to measure nuclear blast waves and radioactive fallout during the Cold War, which dominated the latter half of the 20th century before the ideological conflict thawed in 1989. Monitoring posts such as this one were overseen by the Royal Observer Corps (ROC), who had taken on nuclear monitoring as part of their remit as their aircraft monitoring duties diminished. These posts were designed to withstand a nuclear attack and would hold three to four ROC observers for a minimum of three weeks. Fortified with food and water as well as instruments such as dosimeters and ground zero indicators, posts such as these were important intelligence hubs.

Their subterranean location provided protection for the ROC volunteers from blast and heat, and the effects of radiation would have not been as severe. The volunteers would then communicate with other volunteers at nearby posts for vital information and, with the help of other agencies, disseminate information to the public regarding fallout. The public would then be able to respond to the danger. Almost all the ROC posts were designed by the Home Office and kept to the same design (some had different hatches in parts of the north of England). They became obsolete as tensions dissolved between the East and the West, but many have not been removed due to the cost involved and the difficulty of moving the reinforced concrete. This one was built in 1966 and decommissioned in 1976.

The 350-acre Victory Wood also features a sculpture of naval hero Horatio Nelson and trees planted to reflect his legacy. The Cold War may no longer be the terrifying threat of old, but these structures seek to remind us of the huge challenges and danger of a long, tense conflict.

Address 194 Dargate Road, Yorkletts, CT5 3AH | Getting there 15-minutes from Whitstable town centre via the Triangle bus route from the High Street; Victory Wood car park | Hours Daily 8am – 6pm; take care as some steep slopes and muddy grounds | Tip Eight miles from Canterbury is Sarre House which was fortified in World War II as a defensive strongpoint, strengthened with thick concrete and manned by troops with machine guns.

91_Diver's Helmet

Salvage fashion

No, it's not a particularly shiny method of torture; it's a seaside bow to Whitstable's marine-based gift to the world. Visitors and locals love to stick their head in it for an impromptu photograph besides Whitstable's scenic shoreline. Helmet diving of the kind celebrated here originated in Whitstable in the 1830s. Canvas diving-suited men would dredge the sea for desirables such as metal anchors, guns and even treasure. As with all forms of diving, it could be dangerous, but it could shell out handsome profits. And the Instagram-worthy homes which line Island Wall and Dollar Row were all said to have been built on profits from a salvage by local divers of a slave ship off the coast of Ireland.

Local John Deane, also known as The Infernal Diver, came up with the somewhat surreal apparatus and accoutrements of the trade, inspired by a suit for fire rescue. In the 1830s he led in the salvaging of the wreck of King Henry VIII's *Mary Rose,* sunk in 1545 in a battle with invading French galleys. John and his brother also developed the world's first diving manual, after much research. This detailed manuscript explained the working of the apparatus and how to keep safe under water, which would have come in handy when negotiating Whitstable's bracing seas. Later in his career, John Deane was contracted by the government to clear Russian wrecks from Sevastopol harbour during the bitter Crimean conflict.

If you want to get a feel of some of the booty that Deane and his colleagues would have excavated, a visit to the local museum will bring you up close with period must-haves such as alloy dividers and quatrefoil brooches, as well as the strange and wonderful early diving suits and helmets. And if you've ever thought about trying your lungs out at this tricky yet fascinating pastime, a short stroll away from the silvery sculpture is the local scuba diving club. Tudor artefacts optional.

Address Whitstable Harbour, CT5 1AB | **Getting there** 12-minute walk through town from Whitstable station via Station Road and then through the town in the direction of Harbour Street and then carry on until you reach the harbour; East Quay car park | **Hours** Unrestricted | **Tip** John Deane once lived in Free Diver Cottage, a traditional Whitstable home on Island Wall Road.

92 _Drink Local_
Michelangelo with a social punch

He stalks Whitstable late at night and early in the morning. His weapons are not knives but acrylic paint and a committed social conscience. Stealthily, he daubs his potent messages onto walls around the town. Only doing interviews featuring the back of his head, little is known about him except that he studied locally and lives in the town. Celebrated as 'Catman', he has brought politically tinged street art to a fairly genteel town. One of his most celebrated works is _Drink Local_. It is a depiction of a grizzled and heavily bearded fisherman adorning a spot just off Harbour Street.

Other works to be spied by the mysterious artist include a cheeky Mona Lisa with her thighs showing and a deep-sea diver laden with shopping bags, referencing the town's history as the birthplace of helmet diving. _Shop Local_ is inscribed above it and whilst it may not pack the acerbic punch of a Banksy, to whom he is often compared, street art of any kind is still pretty revolutionary for cosy Whitstable.

Both _Drink Local_ and _Shop Local_ are a call to arms to support the town's independent shops and boozers. These aren't in nearly as much trouble as in the average British town but are still feeling the pinch. Can Catman help them? Only time will tell, but his passion for the town is undoubtedly there and his art is scattered all over Whitstable.

Art abounds in Whitstable, but it is often of an unchallenging bent that depicts such familiar tropes as cutesy beach huts and oyster smacks (fishing boats). Catman's stencils are imbued with Whitstable's spirit but through a contemporary filter, and though he does sometimes veer out to other parts of Kent – and even London – his work has captured imaginations far and wide. Abandoning pointless scrawls, even street art in Whitstable references the town's pride in its quirky shops and pubs. See how many you can spot.

Address Near Flory & Black, 54 Harbour Street, CT5 1AQ | Getting there Visible from Harbour Street, on an unnamed passageway | Hours Unrestricted | Tip Flory & Black is a dreamy interiors shop and exudes Catman's independent spirt (www.floryandblack.com).

93 The Favourite

Everyone's favourite on water or on land

Moored in amongst a forest of shingle flora on Island Wall is the Favourite, one of the town's few remaining oyster yawls, or 'smacks', a small open boat.

Old Favourite, as she is sometimes called, was built in 1890 for Edward 'Pikey' Carden. Fast and nifty, she dredged for young wild oysters and less wholesomely for brandy and tobacco for smugglers. Her trawl would also pull in starfish, crabs and smothering reeds, the latter being marketed to farmers as fertiliser. In 1944 she was machine-gunned by World War II enemy aircraft and put out of commission. Beached and then dragged up the shore, she sat on the shingle for 10 years. In the early 1950s, thanks to the help of several able-bodied seamen, a supply of pink gin and ale and a party atmosphere, local volunteers attempted to move her to a more illustrious resting place. This initial effort failed but a later attempt to bring her to a safe haven succeeded.

For several years, she lay snug beside a cottage owned by London author Harry Hurford-Janes, but faced the threat of neglect once more in the 1970s when he moved. Aided again by the help of locals, this time tempted by free beer and hotdogs, she now rests on Island Wall. The might of Whitstable residents was called on yet again and they campaigned to have her preserved, and her hull was bolstered in an effort to prolong her life. She now sits rather bruised amongst some of the most glamorous properties in the town, but her allure is not lost completely, and she is listed in the National Register of Historical Vessels. Try to imagine her smooth contours setting sail in colourful regattas or gathering the fruits of the sea that had sustained the town since Roman times. It is thought that in her glory years she would have harvested a huge bounty of oysters, helping to keep the town economically afloat. These days, unmoving, she harvests local affection.

Address 28 Island Wall, CT5 1EP | Getting there 8-minute walk from Whitstable station; Keam's Yard car park | Hours Unrestricted | Tip The Smack Inn, originally a pair of fisherman's cottages tucked away on Middle Wall, is a beach-inspired beer garden serving superb food and ales (www.smackwhitstable.co.uk).

94 Fisherman's Huts

A treat in store

Originally brimming with the jangle of the cockle cutters' equipment, these black clapboard huts with bright green shutters were originally referred to by locals as 'stores'. This reflected their larger size than the pastel-coloured beach huts, and they were also considered too attractive to be referred to as sheds. Established around 1869, most probably to fill the void left by the savage fire, in the 1940s they came under the ownership mainly of families who were interested in the leisure of a seaside sail as well as the haul of a trawl. In the 1950s, one enterprising local began to assess how to use them for business and traded yacht fittings on a trestle table outside hers, an endeavour that turned into the original Dinghy Store.

While one store was owned by a local antique dealer, marine usage remained strong. One local owner stored two former oyster smacks putting them to good use to trawl for shrimps. His nets would hang out in the front to dry and anglers and yachtsman would drift in from the sea towards these stores. Not simply a place to store boating equipment, the upper floor would have had a stove for making tea and chairs, fit even for a Coronation party in 1953. Owners did not sleep here though, due to a lack of plumbing.

The buildings eventually became unstable – the antique dealer's store would sway precipitously in the high winds and collapsed in the 1980s – and many were neglected. However, as Whitstable began to bloom again, they were taken over by the Whitstable Oyster Fishery Company, who restored and updated them for a new generation of visitors.

These days they do include plumbing and are holiday accommodation operated by the Hotel Continental. Their distinctive look has been adopted by more recent housing developments such as The Salt Yard referencing their steeply pitched gables and weatherboarding.

Address 3 Sea Wall, CT5 1BX, +44 (0)1227 280280, www.whitstablefishermanshuts.com | Getting there 12-minute walk from Whitstable station via the High Street; Keam's Yard car park | Hours Exterior unrestricted; book online or visit Hotel Continental at Beach Walk for stays | Tip The nearby Whitstable RNLI was established in 1963. It provides access to a viewing platform for a better look of their lifeboat.

95 The *Greta*

Flat-bottomed hulls make the world go round

Its vibrant red sails blowing in the breeze, the graceful *Greta* moored in Whitstable Harbour is a reminder of the time shipping lanes were lit up by these colourful barges. A Thames Sailing Barge, it was built in 1892 and was not simply decorative. This barge was a working ship transporting beer, grain and malt between Essex and the old London docks. Floating on the Estuary, the *Greta* was built in Essex, and is one of only around 30 still in existence today. A true survivor when you consider that it would have been one of around 2000 registered in Britain at the beginning of the 20th century.

The unique design of the barges boosted their popularity. Featuring a flat-bottomed hull, they were one of few vessels to be able to navigate the shallow creeks and thin tributaries of Essex and Kent. At the Horsebridge (see ch. 97), the vessel would have been flat enough to comfortably moor before unloading. These boats would have needed only two people to keep them sailing, with women often among the crew.

Tinged with royalty, the *Greta* once carried the spares for the German Kaiser Wilhelm II's racing schooner. And during World War II, it was commissioned to carry ammunition from the army depot at nearby Rochester to naval vessels anchored in the Thames Estuary. One of the distinct advantages of these barges lay in the fact that they didn't have engines so were perfect for carrying ammunition and explosives. Also, being powered by the hearty local winds, they had no use for the fuel that was much in demand during this time.

During 1940, the *Greta*'s wartime action elevated it further, when it was involved in 'Operation Dynamo', which was the evacuation of British Forces from Dunkirk. The *Greta* can now lay claim to the title of the oldest of the 'Dunkirk Little Ships' still active. With local volunteers determined to maintain her necessary restoration work, the *Greta* still turns heads whatever the tide.

Address South Quay, Whitstable Harbour, CT5 | Getting there 15-minute walk from Whitstable station to the harbour via the High Street and Harbour Street; Harbour car park | Hours Unrestricted viewing between May and October | Tip The sails of World War II American ammunition ship, the SS *Montgomery* can sometimes be viewed from Whitstable's shores. Too dangerous to bring ashore, it is feared that a strong tide could result in it destroying the Isle of Sheppey.

96_Harbour Street

Rising from the ashes

Many serious fires have ripped through Whitstable, and the most devastating one by far occurred in 1869, when flames tore through Harbour Street and its surrounding areas. Around a third of this street's buildings were destroyed, but today this core Whitstable stretch with its gentle curve and narrow spaces is fully alive, brimming with independent shops and historic cafés.

Peep through the crowds to make out the listed buildings, some with their original taxation stamps carved into stone. Just on the brink of Harbour Street is the bright white 18th-century Captain's House, which was inhabited by a local dredgerman. Nearby stand two cottages which are weather-boarded – rendered with a protective layer of wood to guard against the fresh coastal elements. Their sloped mansard roofs feature a distinctive covering of Kent peg tiles. These are smaller than other tiles found in the country, but their irregular shape and warm orange-red colour share countrywide aesthetics.

Run your eyes along the uneven storey heights and roof outlines. Original shopfronts remain intact and contemporary ones blend in. Don't miss the Cheese Box with its informal cheese bar and the legendary Rock Bottom for its selection of unique CDs and vinyl. An inn has stood for over 300 years on the site where the busy Duke of Cumberland stands now; it used to be the headquarters for the town's oyster and dredgermen, and now hosts unmissable music nights.

As for the savage fire, naval officer Captain Jull delivered sermons as the devastating event took hold and with his vision, seeds were sown for the Harbour Church in 1871. It welcomed the fishermen that made up Whitstable's traditional heritage even as the town began to edge towards urbanity in the early 19th century. Yet, the town and Harbour Street's strongly maritime appeal cannot be escaped. Just ask the seagulls.

Address Harbour Street, CT5 1AQ | **Getting there** 12-minute walk from Whitstable station via the High Street and then onto Harbour Street; Gorrell Tank car park | **Hours** Unrestricted | **Tip** You cannot beat the sandwiches and cakes at Tea and Times on the High Street, and you can buy something to read there too from the vast supply of magazines and newspapers.

97 Horsebridge
My town for a horse

Flint tools point to Whitstable having been populated since the Neolithic era, but the town really took shape in 1290 when a sea wall was built ending in Horsebridge. After the Middle Ages, the settlement was referred to as Whitstable Street, with Horsebridge taking centre stage again, and the community liked to be watered here after a tough stint trawling for oysters, working with salt or boat building. By the late 16th century, a number of drinking houses had sprung up amongst the fishermen's cottages and huts near Horsebridge and Harbour Street. Horses and carts would have navigated this slipway, but it also provided mooring for flat-bottomed ships such as Thames barges (see ch. 95) before they made the journey to London and Canterbury with hauls of pottery, oysters and herrings. The fish trade to Canterbury in particular flourished once abbeys and friaries were established at Greyfriars (see ch. 23) and Augustine's Abbey (see ch. 43). Even after Whitstable Harbour was built in 1832, the Horsebridge slipway was still used to transfer cargo, partly because the landing charges were cheaper and Thames barges in particular did not require the deep water of the new harbour.

In view here is a sign for the Company of Free Fishers and Dredgers, an early co-operative established in 1793 and owned by a band of oyster fishermen. It was one of the first forms of limited company recorded and also one of the oldest companies in Europe. After poor harvests in the mid-20th century, oysters began to fade, before facing an even greater threat: the prawn cocktail, which dominated British restaurant menus between the 1960s and 1980s.

The town floundered until 1978, when the Royal Native Stores was revived as a top fish restaurant. Look out also for the Horsebridge Centre with its rotating displays of art and small café with vegan and gluten-free options. No prawn cocktail though.

Address CT5 1AF | Getting there 12-minute walk from Whitstable station via the High Street and Harbour Street; Keam's Yard car park | Hours Unrestricted | Tip It is said that in the mid-19th century you could visit a different pub every week for a year here. There are fewer today, but among the many remaining places is the Old Neptune (or Neppy) – a rare pub on a beach with views of the town's famous sunsets (www.thepubonthebeach.co.uk).

98 Margo Selby Studio

Calculation meets inspiration

Step away from Whitstable's High Street and you will find a determination to take on the understated Scandinavian aesthetic that dominates the town's interior design shops. Textile artist Margo Selby's studio-shop may be small and tucked away but its creativity shouts loudly in a parade of clashing colours and geometric shapes. No one could ever accuse Selby of being a shrinking violet.

Flamboyant rugs, cushion covers and bed linen in luxe silk and practical Lycra are created on-site and upstairs. When you get here, you will be greeted with buckets of remnants that can be bought for a steal. If you're tempted to try and recreate her designs yourself, that's great, but you better get your algebra up to scratch. Weaving is a numbers game. While she has a postgraduate degree from The Royal College of Art, Selby is also something of a geek, proudly proclaiming that maths is pivotal to the foundation of weaving. As she moves deft fingers in a 24-shaft Arm loom she says, 'The mathematical programming of a loom using the binary system is as fundamental to weaving as it is to math and computing.' Eh? Well, she understands and that's all that matters.

Unusually, she champions an ancient technique popular in French and Italian courtly culture, called lampas, alongside her love of maths. Now not so widely practised, she is using these complicated weave structures in a new way to create fun stuff for both home and wardrobe and her resourcefulness and talents know no bounds. London-transplant Selby has taken on the unlikely craft-meets-tech collaboration with brisk enthusiasm. Whether it is designing carpets for local flooring companies or collaborating as a host for the Whitstable Biennale, she has a brought her energies to the forefront of the region's creative scene.

Why not see her weave her maths talent and creativity together for yourself?

Address Bradstowe House, 35 Middle Wall, CT5 1BJ, +44 (0)1227 282758,
www.margoselby.com, info@margoselby.com | Getting there 15-minute walk from
Whitstable station via Cromwell Road and then Harbour Street; Middle Wall car park |
Hours Weaving studio Mon–Fri 10am–5pm | Tip Margo also runs weaving workshops
if you fancy having a go yourself. Information is on her website.

Cushions
Present £20 or 2 for £30
Large £30 or 2 for £50

Throws
Decorative RRP £145/ SALE £95
Woollen SALE £95

99 __ Peter Cushing Bench

The legendary actor's beloved spot

'Hammer horror' veteran and *Star Wars* stalwart Peter Cushing adored his adopted hometown and spent his later years wandering around it as if still on set. Suited and booted, he always tipped his hat to the ladies, and many locals still speak of his generosity and friendliness today even though he died in 1994. He was particularly fond of looking out at the pale waves of the harbour and it is here that you can find a beautiful memorial bench made in Jarrah timber and designed by artist Will Glanfield. Today those seeking Whitstable's very own aura of seaside calm sit there and gaze out to sea in the same manner as Peter Cushing, who loved this very spot and often painted the peaceful sea ebbing away into the distance.

He was also a huge fan of the Tudor Tea Rooms, and let's face it, who isn't? The genteel actor would often stop there for one of their legendary fluffy scones and juicy jams. Underneath the wooden beams of this café you can find a Cushing shrine with photographs and poems he had written. Ask if you can pop round the back of the café to see more of his memorabilia, some of which references his love for the town. He also contributed to local environmental and charitable causes in a typically modest and unflashy manner.

Bizarrely enough for someone who made his name in horror, the Hammer veteran's remains are impossible to find. They were disposed of privately, even spookily, causing something of a controversy. There have been numerous attempts to pinpoint them, but many believe that his ashes were scattered at sea. The mystery of his whereabouts has become something of a local legend. Today, we can only wonder what the enigmatic star might have made of it all. We also wonder what he would have thought of the Wetherspoons named after him, which has retained much of its Art Deco glamour, and the portraits of him dotted around the town depicting him in all his movie star glory.

Address Island Wall, CT5 1EP | **Getting there** Walk down the High Street onto Harbour Street and make your way to the sea; Keam's Yard car park | **Hours** Unrestricted | **Tip** Peter Cushing's adored wife Helen's ashes are interred at Saint Alphege Church in nearby Seasalter. Named after a former Archbishop of Canterbury it was built in the 12th century (www.stalphegeseasalter.org).

100 Playhouse Theatre
A literary landmark

This is a building imbued with literary connotations. A young W. Somerset Maugham wrote about it when it was Chapel College. Maugham lived in the town in the 1880s after an early childhood spent in France. The writer with a fondness for the South Seas found himself in Whitstable with his vicar uncle, after the hammer blow of losing both his parents. The uncle did not extend much love to his nephew, and this probably contributed to the unhappy writer's dim view of the place. He disguises it thinly and disparagingly as 'Blackstable' in both *Cakes and Ale* and *Of Human Bondage* – and historically the town's opinion him of was reciprocated with a general malaise. However, there has been softening towards him thanks to local fans, and you can see portraits of the master of the short story dotted around the town. There have been dedicated literary festivals, alongside plans to raise funds for a mural in his honour.

Today, the building is a theatre, and it hosts a wide variety of talent including local lads Harry Hill and Alan Davies. It is an outlet for the Lindley Players who have been staging productions in the town since the 1940s, performing revues and classic plays, as well as more contemporary offerings. The bright, bold exterior and calm, reflective interior reflect the fact that the theatre is a reconstruction of the United Reformed Church. And yes, there is a ghost. Poor old Shelia, who died on stage (an exit any self-respecting thespian would, yes, die for), is said to be occasionally spied floating amongst the red banquettes and hallowed ceilings of the cavernous interior. As for Somerset Maugham, one of the most popular storytellers of the 20th century crafting tales for print and stage, his spirit remains somewhat neglected by those calling the casting shots. Perhaps a revival should be in order? Lindley Players, we're looking at you.

Address 104 High Street, CT5 1AZ, +44 (0)1227 272042, www.playhousewhitstable.co.uk |
Getting there 10-minute walk from Whitstable station turning onto the High Street
after Railway Avenue; Middle Wall car park | Hours Exterior unrestricted; see website for
productions | Tip The nearby Horsebridge Arts Centre's Somerset Maugham Gallery hosts
rotating exhibitions of visual art (www.thehorsebridge.org.uk).

101 Reeves Beach

A shore place to have fun

This site is recorded by historians as far back as 1604, and until 1794 the area was referred to as 'Lord's waste' – uncultivated communal land, some of which had been a field. Suffering tidal damage, fire and neglect over the centuries, it is today thriving with oyster shacks and parked orange dinghies. The waves lap the shingle shoreline and wooden groynes, and there is little evidence of its chequered past.

With the Reeves Beach name thought to have come into existence via George Reeves, the great-grandson of William Reeves who had a stake in the land in 1794, the beach entered a glamorous phase. In 1913, enterprising George, a local councillor, joined forces with another councillor to purchase the land including the adjacent Warner's land which had been used as a rubbish dump for £2,500 by selling shares to locals. He didn't just stop there. He created a Tudor style tearoom and established an open-air skating rink and indoor roller-skating facilities.

The land buzzed with fairy lights, fancy dress displays and the carnival sounds of a mechanical organ, and flourished until World War I erupted one year later. The conflict impacted on the business and it fell into dereliction. By 1944 the beach was advertised for sale but the main interested party, a Mr Ryan, decided to withdraw his offer of £300 in favour of the council, with 'the property … developed and kept as an open space in the interests of the aged of the town'.

Having experienced several demarcations and ownerships over the centuries the concept of who this land belongs to, with its much sought-after cottages lining the way, began to come under the spotlight in the 1990s. But if you follow the route to Seasalter via the peaceful West Beach, you'll see that the sprigs of sea grass and mallow don't care about shifting and often controversial land rights; in the end nature always blooms.

Address Sea Wall, CT5 1BX | Getting there 12-minute walk from Whitstable station down Station Road and via the High Street; Keam's Yard car park | Hours Unrestricted | Tip The brightly coloured Whitstable beach huts evolved from the bathing machine, which was a similar concept but on wheels. During World War II, many of these huts were removed with rumours suggesting they were deployed for military use.

102 Invicta Steam Engine

Whitstable steams ahead

Where was the world's first passenger railway? Why, here in Whitstable, of course, when the Canterbury and Whitstable Railway opened in 1830. Although rival claims abound, what is not disputed is this railway's claim as the first to take passengers regularly and the first to issue season tickets with a billet handed out in 1834 at Canterbury West Station. Soon, people began referring to the railway as the 'Crab & Winkle', a nickname memorialized today at the popular Crab & Winkle Restaurant in Whitstable Harbour.

Coal and passengers were transported through the Kent countryside, and the line chalked up many railway engineering originals in its wake, including the first modern railway tunnel, sadly inaccessible now. The Invicta steam locomotives were created by Industrial Revolution titan George Stephenson and his son Robert. When the Crab & Winkle line was first proposed in 1824, the directors faced issues with existing locomotives, which were slow and heavy. But the new speedier, lighter engines were a vast improvement. After a period of display at York's Transport Museum, a fully restored Invicta engine from the Canterbury and Whitstable Railway is a centrepiece of the Whitstable Community Museum & Gallery.

Travel to Canterbury before the line had been time-consuming due to turnpiking (collecting money to grant road access) and regular silting of the Stour (see ch. 26). Journey times in the 1830s on the Crab & Winkle were approximately 40 minutes, and by 1846, improvements halved the trip. Now it can take longer to make this journey by car.

The railway was very much a Garden of England endeavour. The line's drivers were said to slow down as the train passed through Blean Woods so passengers could check pheasant traps or pick mushrooms. The Crab & Winkle made its last trip in 1953. Portions of the line were redrawn as a designated cycle route.

Address Whitstable Community Museum & Gallery, 5A Oxford Street, CT5 1AB, +44 (0)1227 264742, www.whitstablemuseum.org, admin@whitstablemuseum.org | Getting there 15-minute walk from Whitstable station via Station Road and Harbour Street in the direction of the sea; Harbour car park | Hours Thu–Sat 10.30am–4.30pm | Tip The 1860 Tollgate Cottage at Borstal Hill remains where the original 18th-century toll gate once stood. A rare reminder of the unpopular toll system, the cottage is still a useful marker for travellers making their way between Whitstable and Canterbury.

103_ Squeeze Gut Alley
Follow in the footsteps of smugglers

Over 20 dark and narrow alleyways link the High Street to the beach, carved into the townscape in the absence of any seashore road.

Canny 18th-century smugglers came to look upon these routes with fondness as they smuggled both contraband and human capital – prisoners of war were bundled through here during the Napoleonic wars. These French prisoners would have suffered in dire conditions in prison ships dotted along the Thames estuary. The lucky ones who escaped would then be brought to London smuggled in on a hoy (a type of small ship regularly plying the north Kent coast) before eventually landing at the low-tide mark near Whitstable. The escapees would then rest up in the town before making their departure via Swalecliffe Rock. Relatives of the prisoners paid handsomely for their safe return. This trade carried on until 1814. Other booty squeezed in by the smugglers included the more usual brandy, tobacco, tea, lace and gin.

The inlets and marshes of the north Kent coast made smuggling simple. Squeeze Gut itself starts off relatively ample for an alleyway before narrowing to a sliver with the daylight poking through before giving way to another alley lined with weeds. Earning its name from naughty youngsters who evaded capture by a local portly policeman, it had previously been known as Granny Bell's Alley, after a grandmother of 16 children who lived nearby. It makes for a fairly dark and musty walk, but its noir charms have not been lost on artist Sophie Brown, who made it a focus for the Whitstable Biennale, inviting participants to walk the alley navigating a sheer voile fabric making this narrow space even narrower. And a local music band have taken the name of the alley for their act, playing dance-worthy blues and rock and roll. Dance in the street – or the alley – but not after too many drinks or you may get stuck.

Address CT5 1EY | **Getting there** 10-minute walk from Whitstable station via Station Road and Harbour Street; Middle Wall car park | **Hours** Unrestricted | **Tip** The Old Brig wreck at nearby Seasalter is so historically valuable it may be granted scheduled monument status. The vessel was thought to have been used by smugglers in the 18th century.

104__ Type 24 Pillbox
We are Invicta

The Thanet Way may be thronged with cars but there are patches of greenery along its sides. Camouflaged amongst these spots, a few metres away from pitstop pub The Long Reach, is a reminder of the area's World War II history. Now an abandoned, moss-spotted structure, in 1940, when Kent was preparing itself for a Nazi invasion, it was a key part of the country's extensive defence network. Around 30,000 of these pillbox defences were constructed but now only about 5,000 remain. A similar one was found nearby and demolished. This one was thought to have been concealed under an earth mound.

During the war this gun emplacement, which would have held eight men, was helmed by volunteers and the Home Guard. You can just make out the slot which inspired the unofficial pillbox name. This etymology emerged during World War I as the resemblance to a pillar-box, as in a post box, was easily comparable. The slit opening recalled these red boxes which were more evident at the time than today. Yet, dispute still surrounds the origins of the pillbox slang. Many support the idea that they owe their name to their visual comparison to medical containers even though not all pill boxes were hexagonal.

Their basic designs were adapted to easily available local building materials, so two pillboxes of the same design could look quite different, but a common thread was that they were all well concealed. This one is easily missed except by the most well-informed locals. As well as pillboxes, keep your eyes peeled for other defence systems such as the pyramid-like dragon's teeth and anti-tank posts.

The camouflaging and design of these structures are still admirable proving ample evidence of Kent's well-planned preparation for a Nazi invasion. Kent bravery and organisation lived up to the official slogan of the county which is Invicta – unconquered.

Address Clapham Hill Road, CT5 3DB | **Getting there** Car or taxi advised, 10 minutes from Whitstable station via B 2205 or A 2990; Long Reach Beefeater car park | **Hours** Unrestricted but not advisable to enter on safety grounds | **Tip** Five minutes away, off-grid Ellenden Farm offers the chance to experience rural Whitstable. Choose from a well-stocked shepherd hut or a bell tent (www.ellenden-glamping-kent.co.uk).

105_V. C. Jones

Come fry with me

You can smell the sizzles from yards away and if that wasn't enough of a giveaway, on Fridays the queues snake down the street. Why is it so popular? Easy – this is fish and chips how it was meant to be. Step into a place with décor that remains largely untouched since its opening in the 1960s and take your seat amongst the crowds for a fishy treat. With morsels saturated in beef dripping, and no plans to update the frying policy for vegan trends, this is food so comforting they may as well wrap you up in a blanket, and portions are so large they struggle to fit on the plate. Ceiling fans spin above the seating area, but the steaminess is hard to contain even in the winter months.

The same family has been peeling the locally grown potatoes for three generations, and the original neon signage welcomes customers from the area and beyond and fans are found all over the world. V. C. Jones has distinguished itself during the 2020 pandemic delivering hundreds of hot meals to elderly and isolating local residents at reduced prices, including free deliveries.

As for the fish, your standard cod and plaice as well as dogfish and skate swim amongst the varieties caught in local waters. With a cheery disdain of anything resembling a healthy option, lunch here is the optimum way to build you up for a hearty walk along the coast. Hot drinks are crowned with whispery froth and come to your table in large mugs. Alcohol is not available.

In the front area of the restaurant there are pictures of the place when it first opened, and a few contemporary interpretations of it by local artists. Much-loved and with little in the way of significant competition, there is no better place in town to settle down with a nice fish supper. With favourable opening times and attractive prices, you could eat here practically every day. . . if your scales could take it.

Address 25 Harbour Street, CT5 1AH, +44 (0)1227 272703, www.vcjones.co.uk, info@vcjones.co.uk | **Getting there** 10-minute walk from Whitstable station via Railway Avenue and Cromwell Road; Harbour car park | **Hours** Tue–Sat 11.30am–8pm, Sun noon–8pm (noon–5pm in winter) | **Tip** The nearby Fishslab Gallery's name references the site's former incarnation but today it serves up art from local talent rather than the local catch (www.fishslabgallery.co.uk).

106_Wheelers Oyster Bar

Dive for pearls in this famed place

The juicy flesh of the oyster tempted the Romans so much that between 78 and 85 AD, slaves were sent to collect them from natural beds at Reculver (see ch. 84). The molluscs were then shipped off to the Roman capital, packed in snow, for the feasts of general Gnaeus Julius Agricola. Julius Caesar's love of oysters is thought to have spurred his invasion plans for these isles. Many, many years later, in 1856, master mariner Richard Leggy Wheeler saw his entrepreneurial chance to capitalise on the plentiful creatures, and opened Wheelers Oyster Bar, right here where it stands today.

Wheelers' Victorian beginnings inspired former local Sarah Waters to set the beginning of her historical novel *Tipping the Velvet* in an oyster bar just like this one would have been in its early days. Oysters weren't seen as a delicacy in that era, however, as evidenced in Charles Dickens' *The Pickwick Papers*, when Sam Weller remarks that 'poverty and oysters always seem to go together'. Cheap and nutritious, they helped to power the labouring population, and hundreds of millions of oysters a year travelled from Whitstable's waters to London's markets. By the end of the 19th century, however, overfishing and pollution had led to the exhaustion of the native beds, meaning that the now-rare oysters were only affordable to the upper classes. Their status as a delicacy remains, although oyster stocks are healthy again.

Wheelers' soft pink building just round from the beach might look cute, but its food is all grown up. Beyond the oysters on offer, the menu includes other luxurious plates such as Kentish smoked chowder and tuna tataki, and you can dine either in the Oyster Parlour or at the Seafood Bar. Not surprisingly, there was once a spate of Wheelers restaurants in London, but none of them had the staying power of the original, now the oldest restaurant in Whitstable. Next time you pass its distinctive pink shell, raise a glass to its part in the town's history.

Address 8 High Street, CT5 1BQ, +44 (0)1227 273311, www.wheelersoysterbar.com, chefmarkstubbs@wheelersoysterbar.com | Getting there 10-minute walk from Whitstable station via Cromwell Road and onto the High Street; Keam's Yard car park | Hours Mon–Tue 10.30am–9pm, Thu 10.15am–9pm, Fri 10.15am–9.30pm, Sat 10am–10pm, Sun 11am–9pm | Tip If it's low tide while you're near the beach, try your hand at fossil (and shark teeth) hunting between Beltinge and Reculver.

107__Whitstable Castle
Dyed in the cliffs

Whitstable Castle was never a defensive structure, despite its name, Gothic style and battlements. Located where Whitstable meets Tankerton, this grand manorial home was once owned by magnate Charles Pearson, who basked in its grandeur.

His good fortune was largely down to copperas, or iron sulphate, which boomed in the 16th century.

Whitstable and Tankerton were once alive with the sulphurous fumes of the thriving – and sometimes hazardous – copperas industry. The coastline's London Clay and cliff recession proved fertile ground for hunting the knobbly nodules that formed copperas. Treated chemically, it formed a green vitriol. After processing, it was used as a versatile fixative dye popular with the clothing industry, tanneries (see ch. 47), ink manufacturers and artists. Management of copperas in the 16th and 17th centuries was tantamount to sitting on a goldmine, and a prime site was found within Tankerton cliffs. Charles Pearson managed several local copperas sites, and his makeshift, hilltop castle, built in the 1790s, included a processing site.

Pearson's business skills did not just benefit him and his growing family, who lived on this grand estate. His acumen also enhanced Whitstable's fortunes. The financial impact of copperas supported the harbour (see ch. 96) and the railway (see ch. 102) in which the shrewd Pearson keenly invested. Never one to shy away from the limelight when the opportunity arose, Pearson even bought himself the title of 'Lord of the Manor of Whitstable'.

This elegant place came under the ownership of many others in subsequent centuries, including a paper magnate, but the black tar of the works can still be seen on the walls today. It is a rare reminder of the site's – and Whitstable's – copperas past. Today, the castle is no longer a residence, but it is a popular wedding venue with tea rooms and well-tended gardens.

Address Whitstable Castle and Gardens, Tower Hill, CT5 2BW, +44 (0)1227 281726, www.whitstablecastle.co.uk/the-castle | **Getting there** 20-minute walk from Whitstable station via Harbour Street and past the Fisherman's Market in the direction of Tankerton | **Hours** Grounds and gardens daily 8am–5pm; tea rooms daily 10am–4pm | **Tip** Salt extraction was another thriving local industry. Extraction from pans on the Seasalter marshes began around 1300. The chef at the village's Michelin-starred The Sportsman Restaurant boils up pans of seawater for local crystals to enhance his innovative dishes.

108_ Whitstable Fish Market
You're whelkome

This buzzing mecca for fish lovers is a must-visit. Also, this market's sustainable seafood policy has been endorsed by the Marine Conservation Society, so go ahead! Dive in! Its fresh offerings include Whitstable's gift to the culinary world: oysters. Harvested on the mudflats of the Thames since Roman times, in 1574 a Royal Patent was granted to the owner of Whitstable Manor for the fishing of the town's oyster beds. While cherished for their fix of pure protein and minerals, too many of them can upset your system. It's unwise to wash them down with spirits. Try them instead the classic way, with prosecco or Champagne.

Although the town is famed for oysters it's also home to another celebrated crustacean – the whelk. Look out for the clear blue eyes of Derrick West, 'The Whelkman', boiling them up to send to London and Birmingham. In his 80s, he may not be Britain's oldest working fisherman, but he must certainly be one of its hardest working. He shuns all thoughts of retirement with a deft prising of a whelk from its shell. This local legend remembers when coal was transported around the harbour by horse and cart. The family business, West Whelks, has been selling their catch for 150 years.

The queues are long for the market's cornucopia of seaside treats, but it is worth the wait. During the summer months the barbecues grilling fresh fish serve up a smoky treat. For more fresh *fruits de mer*, head to the chiller cabinets under the arches of the covered market, which sprang up on the site of the original goods shed of the 'Crab and Winkle' (Canterbury and Whitstable) railway line (see ch. 102). Although the harbour is not the prettiest in the world with various industrial reminders jagging up in the background, it certainly is lively, and smells of the sea. Lobster pots jangle with the day's glossy catch, and the chatter of the fisherfolk in their white overalls rings out.

WHITSTABLE ROCK OYSTERS

£2·00 FOR 1
£10·00 ½ DOZEN

SUSTAINABLY FARMED
LESS THAN A MILE FROM
THE SHORE

BEER
PILSNER
SUNDOWNER
OYSTER STOUT }

½PINT PINT
3·00/6·00

Address Whitstable Harbour, CT5 1AB, +44 (0)1227 771245 | Getting there 12-minute
walk from Whitstable station via Oxford Street and Harbour Street towards the coast;
Harbour car park | Hours Daily 8am–5pm | Tip It's a short stroll to the harbour craft market
selling handmade cards, candles and jewellery, some of which is made of local sea glass.

109__Whitstable Harbour

Shiver me timbers

Whitstable Harbour today is alive with overflowing fish stalls, restaurants and colourful barges. Yet, it was not always such fun. According to local legend, various sorts of sea debris used to wash up at the harbour's Deadman's Corner, including the bodies of the poor souls who perished in the waters. But the name is the only macabre thing about the art infused seating area now.

Despite its spooky name, Deadman's Corner is one of the few places you can sit around the harbour area without buying a coffee. Unveiled in 2011 by locally based architect Roger Seijo, it comprises a 22-metre-long wall made from steel mesh baskets filled with ceramic pebbles. The expansive deck, designed like the bow of a ship to reflect local history, is supported by timber posts that have been built to the same specifications to the groynes (sea defences) that line the shore.

This area has long been a busy location, formerly the site of a railway junction for the loading and unloading of cargo ships in the South and East Quays, with coal being a key and bulky load. The harbour itself was a tidal basin until the first half of the 19th century. It is still very much an industrial harbour with soaring cranes and a large-scale asphalt plant (for creating tarmac). The wind farms in the sea exploit the area's inclement weather – five of the town's windmills had sailed away by the 19th century.

When the harbour was more formally completed in 1832, it became the *de facto* port of Canterbury and the number of boats registered in the town grew by knots. Whitstable began to emerge as a true maritime economy, and by the middle of that century there were at least five shipyards with slipways running down to the sea including Horsebridge (see ch. 97). Despite the commercial and fishing boom, however, seafaring was, and still is, a precarious business – just ask the Deadmen.

Address CT5 1AB | Getting there 15-minute walk from Whitstable station via Oxford Street and Harbour Street in the direction of Tankerton; Whitstable Harbour car park | Hours Unrestricted | Tip Starvation Point at the eastern end of Harbour Street is a triangular piece of land echoing a time when unemployed seamen would congregate here in the hope of being hired for a sea voyage.

110__ Whitstable Yacht Club
This one will float your boat

Whitstable Yacht Club has been drawing sailors in since 1902. They would have first set sail on a mixture of traditional cutters, yawls and lugs. Racers would have also hit the waters of the coast on speedy vessels called Raters. When World War I began, racing was suspended but the club remained open for gentlemen offering more leisurely pursuits and games such as cards and snooker.

After the next war and another suspension, the club bounced back in the 1950s when Rear Commodore 'Slotty' Dawes introduced the first of the new Olympic trapeze dinghies into the UK. Whitstable became the racing centre for these new boats and in 1959 the first ever World Championships held in the UK were held here. These boats were super-fast for the time and radical in that the crew used a trapeze, consisting of a wire from the mast to a belt which enabled them to lie out horizontally with their feet on the side of the boat, to balance the boat against the wind.

Dinghies are preferred by the club today. These vessels can be hauled to the shallow waters of Whitstable and recovered fairly easily. Dinghy racing is something the club organises frequently, and they also hold classes and competitive events on catamarans, windsurfers and skiffs. Casual sailors can also just mess around on the sea without any pressure to race.

If you have around half a day to spare – you can even make your way to the Isle of Sheppey, or perhaps drift around notorious Deadman's Island where coastal erosion has revealed remains believed to be of men and boys who died aboard the prison hulks moored off the Isle of Sheppey over 200 years ago. Sailing also offers the rare chance to independently view the spidery World War II Forts up close, as swimming to them is not advised (see ch. 111). So set sail! The inclusive and friendly club is one of Kent's oldest and has been part of local maritime life since its inception.

Address 3–4 Sea Wall, CT5 1BX, +44 (0)1227 272942, www.wyc.org.uk, offic@wyc.org.uk |
Getting there 12-minute walk from Whitstable station via High Street and then Harbour
Street; Middle Wall car park | Hours If you are not a member then hook up with a friendly
sailor who will let you in the atmospheric Members' bar | Tip At low tide, nearby Tankerton
Beach reveals The Street of Stones, a long, pebbly, natural feature stretching away during low
tide for around 750 metres.

111__ World War II Forts

We fort them on the beaches

Visible looming out of the sea at strategic vantage points off Whitstable and Herne Bay, the Red Sands Fort and the Shivering Sands Fort can bring an eerie chill to a fine day. Springing out of the waters like sci-fi spiders, they were key to World War II defence strategy. Part of army fort clusters designed by Guy Maunsell, they successfully defended the Thames Estuary, gateway to London and heart of Nazi invaders' dreams. While certainly eccentric, Maunsell's designs for these connected platforms for anti-aircraft guns, proved sufficiently effective. Now rusty and abandoned, they are nonetheless iconic along these coasts.

Like the more modern wind turbines, whether you see them at all from the shore very much depends on the weather. Decommissioned in the 1950s, the forts still provide landmark references for ships in the area. Unwieldy concrete and metal structures, they have the look of invading aliens. Not surprisingly, Whitstable's Red Sands Fort was used to good effect in 1968 in the 'Fury from the Deep' episode of the fifth season of *Doctor Who*. Both forts made their mark as short-lived pirate radio stations in the 1960s too. As early as 1959, an attempt to re-float the Red Sands group and bring it ashore was, luckily, defeated by cost. There have been proposals since to demolish it but Project Redsand is a group determined to protect it and, if possible, develop it as a permanent memorial to its historic role.

Shivering Sands Fort over at Herne Bay has also excited creative minds. It featured in a video for the Mystery Jets song 'Bubblegum' in 2016, and in 2005, artist Stephen Turner spent six weeks living alone in its searchlight tower, exploring the theme of isolation. Not that he was that isolated – beneath the waves, fish flock to all the towers for their protective cover. Symbols of war for us, but to the fish they are home.

Address Visible from various points along the coast around Whitstable and Herne Bay | Hours Choose your time via the weather report | Tip If you really want to float up close, you might want to get in training via Whitstable Yacht Club (see ch. 110) and learn to navigate a boat there.

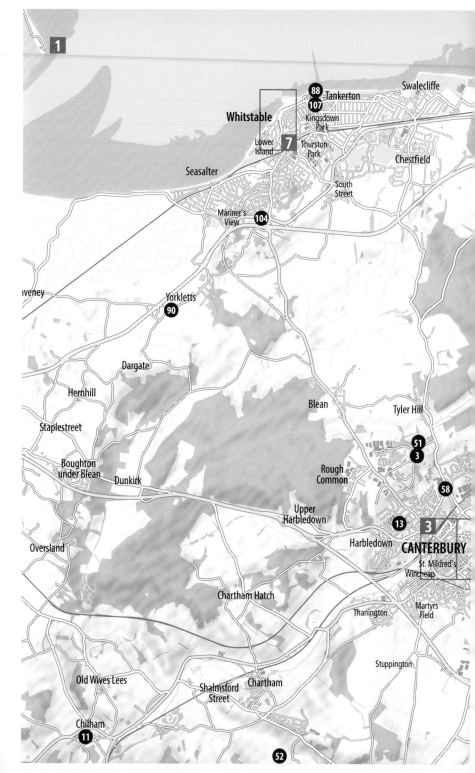

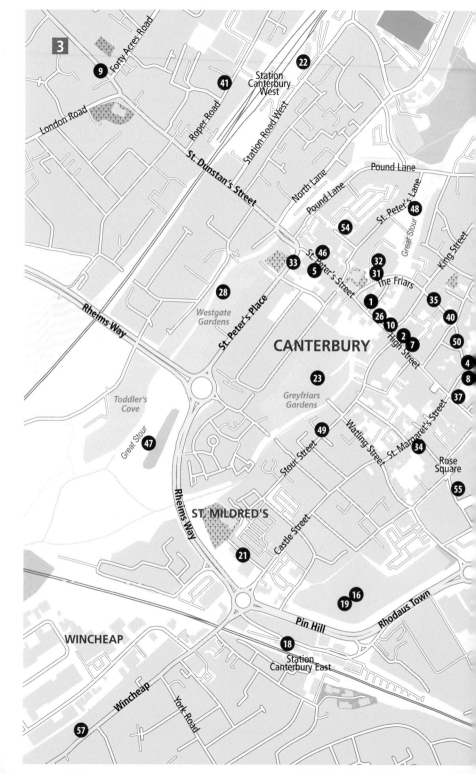

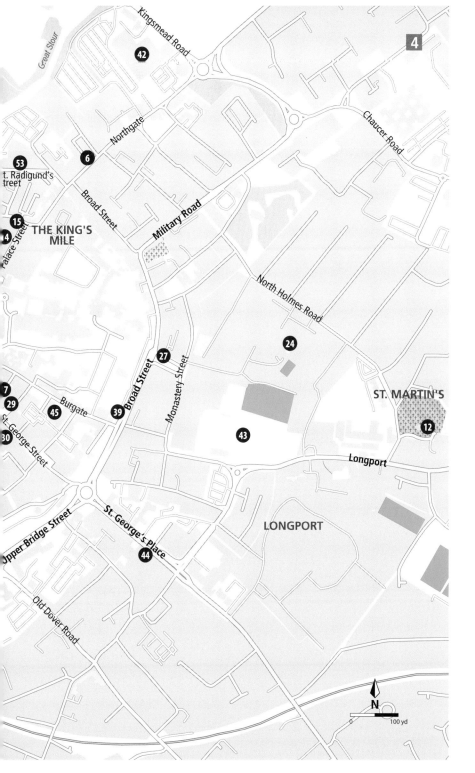

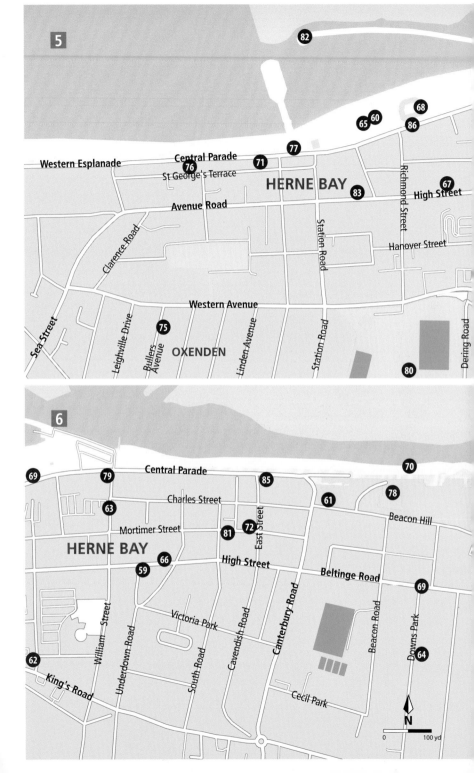

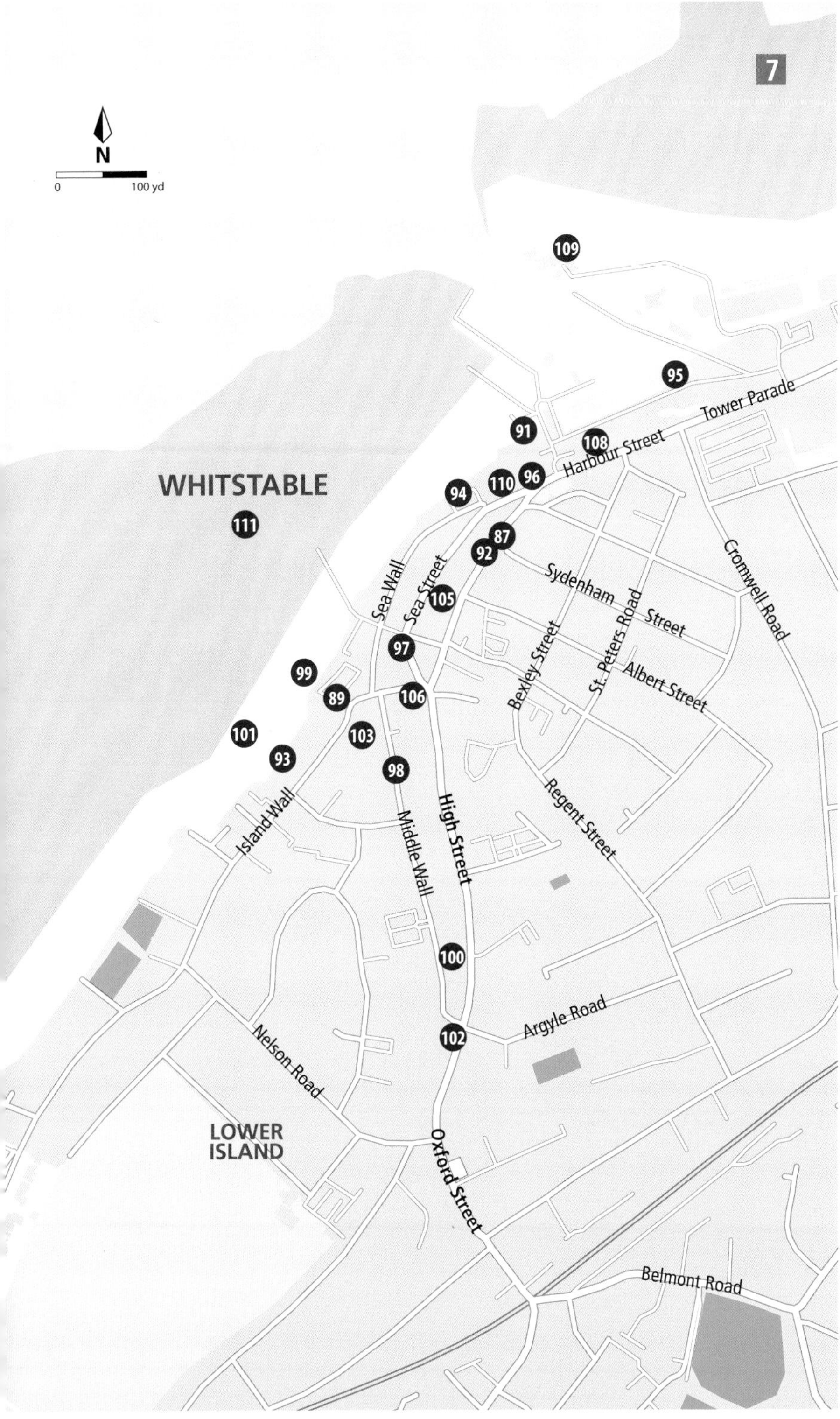

7
N
0
100 yd
WHITSTABLE
LOWER
ISLAND
Tower Parade
Harbour Street
Sea Wall
Sea Street
Sydenham Street
St. Peters Road
Bexley Street
Albert Street
Cromwell Road
Island Wall
Middle Wall
High Street
Regent Street
Argyle Road
Nelson Road
Oxford Street
Belmont Road
87
89
91
92
93
94
95
96
97
98
99
100
101
102
103
105
106
108
109
110
111

Philip R. Stone
**111 Dark Places in England
That You Shouldn't Miss**
ISBN 978-3-7408-0900-3

John Sykes, Birgit Weber
**111 Places in London
That You Shouldn't Miss**
ISBN 978-3-7408-1168-6

David Taylor
**111 Places in Newcastle
That You Shouldn't Miss**
ISBN 978-3-7408-1043-6

Solange Berchemin
**111 Places in the Lake District
That You Shouldn't Miss**
ISBN 978-3-7408-0378-0

Rob Ganley, Ian Williams
**111 Places in Coventry
That You Shouldn't Miss**
ISBN 978-3-7408-1044-3

Martin Booth, Barbara Evripidou
**111 Places in Bristol
That You Shouldn't Miss**
ISBN 978-3-7408-1612-4

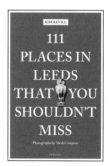

Kim Revill, Alesh Compton
**111 Places in Leeds
That You Shouldn't Miss**
ISBN 978-3-7408-0754-2

Julian Treuherz,
Peter de Figueiredo
**111 Places in Manchester
That You Shouldn't Miss**
ISBN 978-3-7408-0753-5

Michael Glover,
Richard Anderson
**111 Places in Sheffield
That You Shouldn't Miss**
ISBN 978-3-7408-0022-2

Acknowledgments

Thanks to Nichola Jarvis for nourishing me, Julie Dean for constant encouragement, Clive Paul Jackaman for making me laugh and Margaret Gaskin for clear-headed editing and friendship. Most of all I would like to thank Maria for her strength and love. I also thank my sister Christina and Maria's carers especially Binta, Lillian, Charlie, Stuart, Bliss and Alex and Lisa.

Many kind professionals and enthusiasts gave their time and knowledge when it came to researching this book. They include: Enid Allison, John Andrews, Lauren Baker, Peter Banbury, John Barcham, Karen Baxter, Paul Bennett, Len Bennett, Rebecca Booth, Craig Bowen, Rose Broadley, Holly Buggins-Eaves, Shaun Butler, Michael Carter, Emma Cripwell, Liz Crudgington, Rosanne Cummings, Jackie Davies, Matt Demedts, Chris Denham, Sandra Drew, Martin Dixon, David Townsend, Jackie Eales, Colin Elliott, Kathryn Ferry, Elizabeth Finn, Robert Fleming, Margaret Gaskin, Eve Gaut, Roger Green, John Grigsby, Mark Harrison, Sam Holland, Judi James, Dan Jones, Matthew Jarvis, Elizabeth Machin, Stephen Melton, Christopher Paveley, Michael H Peters, Philip Robinson, David Spooner, Caroline Stockmann, Sarah Munday, Imogen Morrell, Steve Norris, Margaret Patterson, Roy Porter, Steve Porthcmouth, David and Pat Roberts, James Roberts, Julia Seath, Ian Stead, Shelia Sweetinburgh, Professor Vanessa Toulmin, Mandy Troughton, Kathryn Tye, Julie Wassmer, Sarah Waters, Deborah Walsh, Dr Helen Wicker, Leo Whitlock, Ian Wild

Nicolette Loizou was born and is based in Kent and studied at the London College of Communication. She loves writing about travel and has contributed to *The Guardian*, *South China Morning Post* and *The Independent* after many years of hot-footing it around the world. She is a big fan of Kent and its varied sights and sounds and loves the region for its laid-back charm and huge variety of things to do. When she is not writing she likes cooking and going to see live bands.